HARTFORD PUBLIC LIBRARY

The Pipe Book

THE PIPE BOOK

A History and How to

by William Goldring

 DRAKE PUBLISHERS INC   NEW YORK

Published in 1973 by
Drake Publishers Inc.
381 Park Avenue South
New York, N.Y. 10016

© William Goldring, 1973

ISBN 0–87749–426–6
LCCCN 72–10527

Printed in the United States of America

Contents

I   ON THE TITILLATION OF NOSTRILS
      or   THE DRY DRINK DENUDED..1

II   PRECEDENTS AND PRECURSORS..........................12
       Getting Back to the Earth...13
       The Cloud Blowers..17
          How to make a tube pipe...20
          How to smoke a tube pipe..22
          How to make a baubau..25
          How to smoke a baubau..25
       Eskimo Pipes..27

III   INDIANS OF THE VALLEYS AND PLAINS...............30
       Mound Pipes..31
       Calumet: the Pipe of Peace...33
          How to make kinnikinnik (Indian tobacco)................35
          How to make a calumet..41

IV   HOOKAHS AND HUBBLE-BUBBLES.......................48
       The Nargeeleh..49
          How to make a nargeeleh.......................................50
       Chinese Water Pipes...54
       The Hookah...56
          How to make a hookah..57

V   SIX SMOKING PIPES...68
       Clay..69

Cherrywood..73
    How to make a cherrywood pipe..73
Meerschaum...78
    The meerschaum fancier's ten commandments.....................81
Briar...83
    How to make a briar pipe...86
    Good Things To Know (about a briar pipe)..........................94
Porcelain..98
Corncob..100
    How to make a corncob pipe...101

VI   NINE CURIOUS CONTEMPORARIES........................104
A Multiple-passage Tree Pipe...105
Two Dowel Pipes...107
A Free-form Standing Pipe...109
A Chem-lab Hookah..110
A Wood Or Stone Hasheesh Pipe...110
A Water Pipe Just For Roaches..114
Two Makeshift Pipes...116

VII   A WORD ON TOBACCO...120

SELECTED SPECIALTIES AND ODDITIES............................128

PREFACE

by Henry Brown

There's clay pipes an' briar pipes an' meerschaum pipes as well;
There's plain pipes an' fancy pipes—things jes made to sell:
But any pipe that can be bought for marbles, chalk, or pelf,
Ain't ekal to the flavor of th' pipe you make yourself.

Jest take a common corn cob an' whittle out the middle.
Then plug up one end of it as tight as any fiddle;
Fit a stem into th' side an' lay her on the shelf,
An' when she's dry you take her down, that pipe you made yourself.

Cram her full clar to th' brim with nachral leaf, you bet—
'T will smoke a trifle better for bein' somewhat wet—
Take your worms and fishin' pole, and a jug along for health,
An' you'll get a taste of heaven from that pipe you made yourself.

Composed in 1896

ON THE TITILLATION OF NOSTRILS
or
THE DRY DRINK DENUDED

"They also have a tree," the ancient text reads, "which bears the strangest produce. When they are met together in companies they throw some of it upon the fire round which they are sitting, and presently, by the mere smell of the fumes which it gives out in burning, they grow drunk, as the Greeks do with wine. More of the fruit is then thrown on the fire, and, their drunkenness increasing, they often jump up and begin to dance and sing. Such is the account which I have heard of these people."

This excerpt, taken from Herodotus' account of a certain Scythian tribe, was written in the fifth century B.C. Today, many archeologists and anthropologists believe it was Indian hemp or *Cannabis sativa* that Herodotus called "the strangest produce." But no matter what intoxicating fruit these tribesmen burned, the narrative does suggest that smoking, in one form or another, is at least 2500 years old. Like singing and dancing, it is a sort of ceremony that has survived from the earliest times—another example that the threads of the past are indelibly woven into the the cloth of the present.

Pipe smoking, of course, is a refinement. Instead of inhaling fumes from an open fire, "civilized" people began drinking their smoke through tubes of clay—for so smoking was called when, toward the close of the

sixteenth century, if first became fashionable in Europe. The term 'drinking' derives from the Spanish conquistadors who, observing the Aztecs swallow their smoke, could think of nothing so suitable to describe this unprecedented phenomenon. Tobacco, consequently, was known as 'the dry drink', and both terms were used commonly until the middle of the seventeenth century.

In an age so decidedly dandyish as Elizabeth's, the novelty of smoking won immediate and affectionate attention. From the moment Columbus discovered "men with half-burnt wood in their hands and certain herbs to take their smokes," until a century or so later when Barnaby Rich would report the establishment of "7000 houses- . . . that trade of selling tobacco" in and around London, the appeal of smoking, and of tobacco in particular, was genuine and pervasive.

By 1600, professors of the "art of whiffing" were nailing up their notices, or advertisements, about London. These so-called tobacco tutors would, for a fee, instruct their clients in "the most Gentlemanlike use of Tobacco." Pipe smoking, no less than another custom of that day, courting, had become a true discipline—replete with rites, tricks and correct etiquette.

Before any young gentleman, or gallants as they were affectionately called, would presume to take his first whiff in public, there were certain rudiments with which he had to familiarize himself: the how, when and where of whiffing. Women, for instance, were easily offended by these "fume suckers" (though it has been said that Queen Elizabeth herself enjoyed an occasional puff with the chivalrous Sir Walter Raleigh). However, after a fortnight of professional tutelage, an initiate could hope to have perfected

his technique as well as his ability to prudently avoid any *faux pas.*

Deft tricks such as the *Cuban Ebolition*, the *Corollary* and the *Whiffe* were mastered. Presumably used to produce various effects with the smoke (i.e., wreaths, curls, rings, fans, etc.), these and other specialties have unfortunately disappeared from usage. One prodigiously difficult trick, however, is related by Ben Jonson, the playwright and eminent Elizabethan. This involved receiving "the 1, 2, and 3 Whiffe, if it please him, and (upon the receipt) take his horse, drink his three cups of Canary, and expose one [puff] at Hounslow, a second at Stares, and a third at Bagshot." What made this feat so extraordinarily difficult was the fact that the three villages were separated each by a distance of several miles.

" . . . let him show his several tricks in taking it, as the whiff, the ring, etc., for these are compliments that gain gentlemen no mean respect."
from The Gull's Horn-book (1602)

Once the apprenticeship was successfully maneuvered, it was next necessary to acquire the proper equipment, without which no true tobacconist could satisfactorily enjoy his smoky recreation. First and foremost, a full batallion of clay pipes, some decorated with gold or silver, was essential. Stored safely in a fitted case, a dozen was deemed adequate. Tobacco was kept in a box, preferably one of ivory which often had a capacity of up to a full pound. Twisted in long rope-like strands, it had to be painstakingly shredded. A special knife and a thick plank of maple called a trencher readied the tobacco for the

The Chivalrous Sir Walter Raleigh

Twisting Roll Tobacco

pipe. Then, because the tobacco was usually too damp, a small shovel or scoop aerated and dried the shredded leaves. Suitable at last, the tobacco was packed into the bowl by a stopper or rammer, some adorning the hand as finger rings. Opulently designed, they are true period pieces and sought after by both museums and private collectors.

Ready to light up, the convenience of the ordinary match uninvented, a burning ember of aromatic juniper wood was set atop the tobacco and gradually combustion ensued. For this operation, a pair of ember-tongs were invaluable. Finally, after a refreshing whiff, a metal pick facilitated the loosening of the ash and cleansing of the bowl.

Unquestionably, it was a discipline that required technical proficiency of a special ilk. In the seventeenth century interlude entitled *Wine, Beere, Ale, and Tobacco Contending for Superiority*, translated from the Dutch by Mercurius Brittanicus "for the benefite of his Nation," a rather satirical synopsis of the art is offered:

1. Take your seal
2. Uncase your pipe
3. Draw your box
4. Produce your rammer
5. Blow your pipe
6. Open your box
7. Fill your pipe
8. Ram your pipe
9. Withdraw your rammer
10. Return your rammer
11. Make ready
12. Present
13. Elbow your pipe
14. Mouth your pipe
15. Nose your tobacco
16. Give fire
17. Puff up your smoke
18. Spit on your right hand
19. Throw off your loose ashes
20. Present to your friend
21. As you were
22. Cleanse your pipe
23. Blow your pipe
24. Supply your pipe

In numerous instances, it was actually this sort of fanfare that first appealed to the urbane sensibility, providing it with an altogether new and beguiling diversion. Albeit, it would be a terrifically unfair assertion to attribute its appeal solely to this factor.

The exploration of the New World

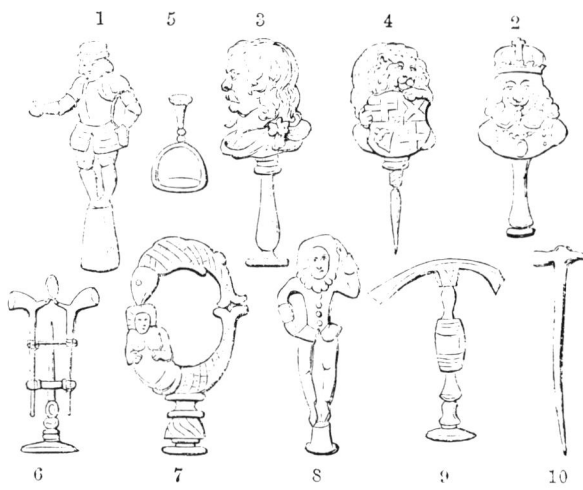

Some Opulent Rammers, Two of Which Were Worn as Finger Rings

An Elizabethan Tobacco Shop

"*The Old World was sure forlorn / Wanting thee!*"

Charles Lamb

Curiously enough, this was the introduction of tobacco into Europe. Its story—a tribute to man's misconceptions as well as his proclivity to perfection—in generous measure contributed to the appeal of smoking across the continent. This is what happened.

The Indians of North America, believing that tobacco was a divine gift, revered it as an integral part of their spiritual community. Dried leaves of the plant, for instance, were set at the foot of waterfalls and other natural wonders which, they fancied, were the abodes of certain gods. Faraway dieties, the Great Spirit included, were pacified and entreated to by smoking. United with fire, a spiritual entity unto itself, tobacco seemingly ascended to the heavens. Also, because in primitive societies religion and medicine so often sprang from the same spiritual well, tobacco was used as a curative and general restorative. Consequently, when the Europeans learned of this fantastic plant, they encouraged the profitable utilization and assimilation of it into their own culture.

In the oddly titled *Breeding of Worms in Human Bodies* occurs one account of its many virtues. Tobacco produces, its author asserts, "such a Tranquility in the Body and Mind, that we may look upon this plant as the famous Herb mentioned by Homer, that had the Virtue to change Sadness into Joy; for Tobacco, by the power of its Sulphur, dissipates Grief or Heaviness, makes People sensibly happy in the midst of Poverty."

Inventive and feverishly ardent, physicians of the age contrived oodles of ways in which tobacco might be dispensed. There

touched the Old at principal latitudes of thought, geographical and metaphysical. Old conceptions were disproved, disrupted or, at least, subject to dispute; it was a real and violent metamorphosis. Enchanted by that fair and savage land, the Old World was easily impressed by it and susceptible to its influence. Consequently, when reports of "a happie and holy herbe" used by the natives with incredible results reached their cities, the Europeans celebrated the discovery of a panacea or cure-all. It could heal wounds, stave off hunger and thirst, prevent disease and appease the pagan gods (or so claimed the reports). In 1561 the French ambassador to Portugal, Jean Nicot, sent some of the herb to Catherine de Medici, Queen of France. It cured her crippling headaches and, to honor her ambassador, she proclaimed it *Nicotiana*.

New World Savages Drinking Tobacco Broth, Smoking Tobacco from a Pipe and Inhaling Tobacco Fumes from an Open Fire   Engraving by Jacques Le Moyne De Morgues (d. 1588)

were tobacco pills, plasters and poultices; oils, unguents and infusions; salts, essences, extracts, tinctures and balms. These and other analagous "remedies," they supposed, could cure a list of ailments as long as the proverbial arm. A scant sampling includes boils, hiccoughs, trembling limbs, jaundice, imbecility, tooth and ear aches, pleurisy, dyspepsia, dysentery, dysuria, lethargy, corpulence, giddiness, dropsy, ringworm, halitosis, syphylis, carbuncles, chilblains and even "general lousiness." During the years 1664–1666, when the Great Plague ravaged London and its environs, tobacco waxed exceedingly popular as a preventative. Tobacco smoke, it was conjectured, purged the body while immunizing it against infection. For this reason, schoolchildren at Eton were required to take a few whiffs of the pipe every morning.

Another precaution is recorded in the *Diary* of Samuel Pepys. The seventh of June, 1665, was "the hottest day that ever I felt in my life. This day . . . I did in Drury Lane see two or three houses marked with a red cross upon the doors, and 'Lord have mercy upon us!' writ there [quarantine]. It put me in an ill conception of myself and my smell, so that *I was forced to buy some roll tobacco, to smell it, and chaw,* which took away my apprehension." Chewing tobacco was considered an excellent purge, and its approval in 1614 by the Scottish physician William Barclay set a precedent for this sort of therapy. To cure "an armie of maladies," he advised inserting a round ball of tobacco leaves "of such bignesse that it may fill the patient's mouth." Presently, "there shall flow such a flood of water from his brain and his stomacke . . . that it shall be a wonder." Not unlike blood-letting, this practice operated on the body's evil humours; if you were "full of evil humours," the doctor recommended, "do this once a week, otherwise once a month."

Certainly one of the most eccentric *modus operandi*, the Clyster-pipe was a tobacco smoke enema. "Being taken backward," praised one physician, " 'tis excellent good against the colic." Used extensively for intestinal disorders, the Clyster-pipe was condoned by James I. Otherwise a fierce anti-tobacconist, he "merrily said this was the way to take it."

Tobacco's reputation as a panacea, however, was not strictly confined to purgative pursuits. Indeed, its supposed potency found countless applications. In 1633, one physician instructed "those cold and inept in the cause of love" to use it as an aphrodisiac. "It is so beneficial," said another, "that loving husbands should persuade their wives to adopt the habit. Tobacco helps procreation and prevents the birth of weak children." A contemporary, Saint Joseph of Cupertino, held the opposite conviction. Tobacco, he opined, was actually an anti-aphrodisiac. "Taken in moderation," he said, "tobacco is not only useful but even necessary for preachers, monks, brothers and other religious who ought and desire to lead a chaste life and repress sensual emotions . . . therefore," he concludes, "tobacco should not be used by married people."

A report in *The Country Farme* (1616) contends that the tobacco ash is equally useful. "You shall understand," its author asserts, "that the ashes of this Nicotiana is of no less sovereignty and medicinal use than the leaf . . . for after you have taken the fume of tobacco, and that the powder is burnt into ashes, you shall save those ashes in a closed box, for they will cure any green wound whatsoever, and if you steep them in white wine or urine and make a lee thereof (but urine is the better because it has a certain oily substance in it which comforteth and suppleth sores), and with this lee if you bathe any old inveterate ulcer, it will take away the itch, cleanse it and heal it. If with these ashes also you rub your teeth, it will make them white and smooth and preserve them a long time from rotting."

Tobacco stirred the imagination and inspired creativity. It is not surprising, therefore, to find the poetry of the epoch venerating it. In the *Fairy Queen*, for example, Spenser sends his Belphoebe

Into the woods hence-forth in haste she went,
To seeke for herbes that mote him remedy;
For she of herbes had great intendiment,
Taught of the Nymph which from her infancy
Had nursed her in true nobility:
There whether it *divine Tobacco* were,
Or Panachea, or Polygony,
She found and brought it to her patient deare,
Who all this while lay bleeding out his heart-blood neare.

One exceptional artistic endeavor, however, excells all others: *a tobacco ballet*. It was executed by a group of Portuguese in the seventeenth century. Fairholt, the antiquarian, tells us "the scene was laid in the island of Tobago, the supposed native place of tobacco, and a troop of its inhabitants were introduced chanting in celebration of the good fortune of people to whom the gods had granted a plant so precious. Four priests, taking tobacco in powder from golden boxes pendant from their girdles, cast it in the air to appease tempests. The rest then marched in solemn procession round their idols, with long pipes in their mouths, fumigating them as with incense. A second scene exhibited manufacturers at work, tying up leaves of the plant, cutting it for the smokers and pounding it for the snuff takers. The third and last scene introduced the customers of the herb, and a general dance, in which all mixed together and offered pinches from each other's snuff boxes. The smokers of all nations, in appropriate costume, joined the dance, to indicate the reunion of all peoples and creeds under the powerful influence of tobacco; the natives leaping among them all till the curtain fell."

Despite its evident appeal, tobacco did attract a violent and vocal opposition: the anti-tobacconists. The conflict, originating in the anti-tobacconist conviction that tobacco was "a pestiferous and wicked poison from the devil," focused on issues formerly extolled by its enthusiasts. Whereas tobacconists declared it assisted procreation, for instance, anti-tobacconists contended that "it withereth and drieth up natural moisture in our bodies, thereby causing sterility and barrenness: in which respect it seemeth an enemy to the continuance and propagation of mankind."

Then as now, it was smoking in particular that incurred anti-tobacconist hostility. In his famous *Tobacco Battered*, Joshua Sylvester goes so far as to propose that the tobacco pipe is more lethal than a gun. "Two smoky engines," he holds, "have been invented in this our age: guns and tobacco pipes, of which the latter is the more deadly and infernal. For guns shoot forward at the foe, but tobacco pipes attack their own, poisoning their users. And if tobacconists keep on their course, they can better endure hell's sulphuric smoke."

Coining such phrases as "the filthie fume" and "the precious stinke," they all rallied behind King James I. A staunch hater of smoking, he penned this oft-quoted observation in his *Counterblaste to Tobacco*. Smoking, he advances, is "a custom loathsome to the eye, hateful to the nose, harmful to the brain, dangerous to the lungs and, in the black stinking fume thereof, nearest resembling the horrible Stygian smoke of the pit that is bottomless." Sensational, exhaustive and vehement, the *Counterblaste* actually did little to retard the popularity of 'the dry drink'. Puffing did persist, tobacco prevailed and even a king's harangue could not avert its dispersion.

In the aforementioned seventeenth century interlude, Tobacco, who is cast as "a swaggering Gentleman," contends that his "divine breath doth distill eloquence and oracle upon the tongue." Boasting too that he is already acknowledged "a heavenly quintessence, a divine herb, a sovereign drink," he petitions Wine, Beere and Ale to accept him into their fraternity of mirth. Wine, the sagacious, concedes: "This ruffler may be troublesome; we were best to admit him to our society; he is a dry companion, and you may observe how he hath insinuated already with in which Ponce de Leon set out to find a Fountain of Youth; it was the age that explored and exploited most of the known world. It was the age in which an omnipotent queen's chief counsellor was her astrologer; it was the age of Galileo. It was the age that composed polite light verse; it was the age of Donne and Shakespeare. It was the age that cheered and jeered as thousands of tobacconists lit their pipes in public; it was the smoking age.

* *

King James I, Author of the Counterblaste

the greatest; the ladies begin to affect him, and he receives private favors from their lips . . . when he appears in a fair pipe; for our own sakes, let us hold correspondence with him, lest he seduce men to forsake us.'' So settled, Wine, Beere and Ale ''doth enter into league with Tobacco.''

> "One cleares the braine, the other glads the hart."
> *from an Elizabethan ditty*

Certainly it was an auspicious age for the introduction of 'the dry drink'. It was the age

It used to be, Fairholt tells us, that in Germany one could discern a man's disposition simply by his puffing. "They have the puff acquiescent, the puff dissentient, and the puff doubtful. The puff acquiescent is given downwards, from a small round apeture formed in the center of the lips accompanied by a slight inclination of the head forward; the puff dissentient, on the contrary, is given upwards; the body thrown slightly back, the chest expanded, and the column of smoke broader and somewhat more vehement. For the puff doubtful, the

head is slightly inclined toward the right shoulder, and from the left corner of the mouth curls gently upwards, as fine as a cobweb, this dubious whiff."

Then even as now, you *are* how you puff, no less than *what* you puff or *from* what you puff; these are the true delights of the art. To the eighteenth century lexicographer Samuel Johnson, a pipe was but "a tube of clay through which the fume of tobacco is drawn into the mouth." However, a pipe is more than that, for, as Haliburton happily observed, "it's the poor man's friend; it calms the mind, soothes the temper, and makes a man patient under troubles. It has made more good men, good husbands, kind masters, indulgent fathers and honest fellows, than any other blessed thing on this universal world."

PRECEDENTS AND PRECURSORS

Getting Back to the Earth

There is convincing evidence that the avocation of smoking, even as it proceeds today, has evolved from an instrinsic need of the soul. In his *De Fluvius*, Plutarch tells the tale of a plant that is found near the river Hebrus. "The inhabitants of that country," he continues, "throw the leaves on a brazier and inhale the smoke, which intoxicates them." This account, comparable to that of Herodotus, reveals an early disposition to intoxication. This longing, no less prevalent now than in ancient times, is a priority of life.

By inhaling the smoke of certain plants, our predecessors discovered that a desirable state could be induced. Writers like Plutarch and Herodotus testify to their indulgence. Inevitably, the art of whiffing developed as an adjunct to the pursuit of intoxication.

In 1526, Oviedo described one of the Indian's evil practices. "In order to produce a state of stupor," he states, "the *caciques* [priests] employed a tube, shaped like a Y, inserting the forked extremities in their nostrils and the tube itself in the lighted weed; in this way they would inhale the smoke until they became unconscious and lay sprawling on the earth like men in a drunken slumber." Later on, he adds that "they prize this herb very highly." The herb, of course, was tobacco, the Y-shaped tube one of the earliest sophistications of the art.

Although a trifle uncouth, the Y shape is one of the most expedient and efficacious devices for intoxication ever contrived, but used as a sort of tool, the nose pipe actually assisted the *cacique* in his occupation. Called on to provide direction for the perplexed, he had recourse to it often. In his *Joyous News* (1580), Monardes describes the priest's procedure:

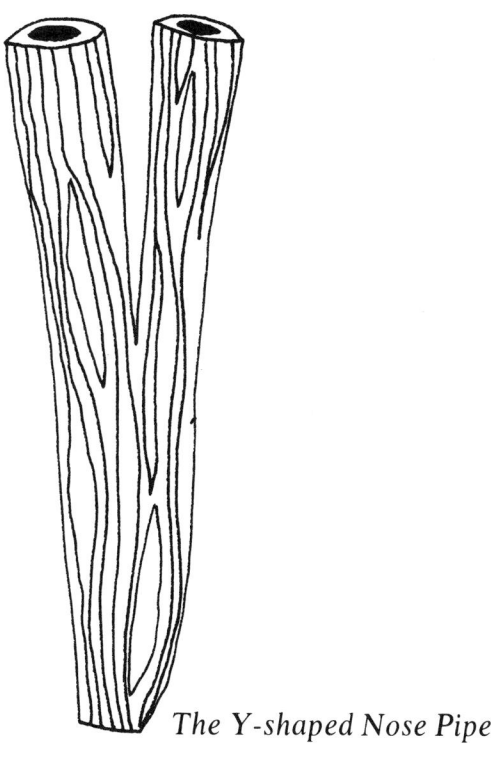
The Y-shaped Nose Pipe

When there was amongst the Indians any manner of business, of great importance, they went and propounded their matter to their chief Priest, forthwith in their presence, he took certain leaves of the Tobacco, and cast them into the fire, and did receive the smoke of them . . . at his nose with a Cane, and in taking of it, he fell down upon the ground, as a Dead man, and remaining so, according to the quantity of the smoke he had taken, when the herb had done his work, he did revive and awake, and gave them their answers, according to the visions and illusions which he saw, while rapt in the same manner, and he did interpret to them.

Intoxication by tobacco no doubt strikes today's reader as exceedingly odd, but if one considers the huge quantities these natives consumed at one sitting, it can be readily understood: *four or five handfuls was not at all unusual.* Of course, in lands in which tobacco was not introduced until after the Discovery—principally Africa and Asia—*dakka, bhang* or, as it is called here, marijuana was smoked. Interestingly enough, after its introduction to these lands, tobacco frequently had the distinction of being the preferred smoke.

TRY THE WEED!

Jupiter, try the weed!
—Edward Bulwer, Lord Lytton

Different folks, it can be said, like different smokes. So, too, do they like different devices whereby to take their smokes, but, as vast and diverse as the continents of

> *He who doth not smoke hath either known no great griefs, or refuseth himself the softest consolation, next to that which comes from heaven. "What, softer than woman?" whispers the young reader. Young reader, woman teases as well as consoles. Woman makes half the sorrow which she boasts the privilige to sooth. Woman consoles us, it is true while we are young and handsome: when we are old and ugly, woman scolds and snubs us. On the whole, then, woman in this scale, the weed in that, Jupiter, hang out thy balance, and weigh them both; and if thou give the preference to woman, all I can say is, the next time Juno ruffles thee—O*

Africa and Asia undoubtedly are, there was one curious custom that once bound them together closely: the practice of *earth smoking.* Be it *dakka,* tobacco, or betel leaves, all indulged in this crude yet durable fashion.

Earth smoking can be divided into its three levels of development. In its simplest, it was practiced in the prone position, the smoker stretched out full length upon the earth. The device, though nothing but a tightly packed heap of earth, was actually the first true pipe: it had a bowl—a depression in the top of the heap—and a stem—a subterranean channel fashioned by withdrawing a reed purposely left embedded in the heap. To attest to its durability, though this is the earliest aboriginal level, it was actually used by Indian soldiers during World War I.

Earth-smoking at Its Simplest: Primitive and Prone

Called the *cajote* in Africa, the next level of earth smoking was evidently innovated in a spirit of hospitality, for it is the first pipe whereby friends could invite friends to share a bowlful. The technique is here described by an observer of the Kirghis Tartars in 1788. He declares:

The natives employ a very primitive method: one of them urinates to make the ground firm and air-tight, a hole is then made at that spot and it is filled with tobacco. The tobacco is lighted and each of the smokers inserts obliquely the dried stem of a hollow reed into the ground, and thus they obtain the desired smoke.

As another account evinces, the number of participants is nearly limitless. In South America, one scholar claimed, there lived a tribe called the Ogatopoks who smoked a "monster pipe." A typical *cajote* but for its enormity, "this huge pipe is surrounded at one time by a hundred to a hundred and fifty aspirants, who fix their long tubes of reed into the numerous holes with which its sides are bored."

Popular in native circles, the *cajote* also had the distinction of having a fraternity named after it in the seventeenth century. The story goes that several French officers were dining at an inn near Hanover one day, and after their supper they each proceeded to ready a pipeful. An officer who had served in Africa, however, proposed that they smoke in the tribal mode, and he led his fellows outside. There he constructed a *cajote*, and after an hour or so, they were so delighted that they decided to found a fraternity to honor this splendid and friendly device. And so it was that the Knights of the *Order of the Cajote* puffed themselves into existence.

Despite this distinction, the *cajote* still has one serious defect: It is stationary. It cannot be carried about and is likely to be eroded by wind and rain. Making it mobile, however, sacrifices its friendly countenance, its unique ability to service a houseful of smokers. Nevertheless, this was the next level of earth smoking: the personal, portable pipe.

Of this type, there are two possibilities: the earthen and the reed. The earthen pipe is really nothing but the heap type excavated. Usually fabricated from mud, then sun- or oven-dried, these pipes made sturdy companions on long trips. Beside the convenience of not having to stretch out to smoke it, a new one need not be built each night. A further refinement, the reed pipe need not even be lifted to the lips as the earthen. It is the final innovation of the type and provides a refreshing whiff with no effort save the lighting of it. The traveler William Bosman described such a pipe in 1705.

Some of them [West Africans] have Pipes made of Reeds, which are about six foot long; to the end of which is fixed a Stone or Earthen bowl, so large that they can cram in two or three handfuls of Tobacco; which Pipe thus filled they without ceasing can easily smoke out; and they are not put to hold their pipe, for being so long it rests on the Ground.

Lighting a six-foot pipe, however, can be particularly awkward without assistance. In fact, either a servant or friend is needed.

All in all, the portable pipe irrevocably recast the smoking customs of these peoples. Still hospitable, the natives could still invite their friends to share a pipe. But now, instead of all inserting their reeds into a

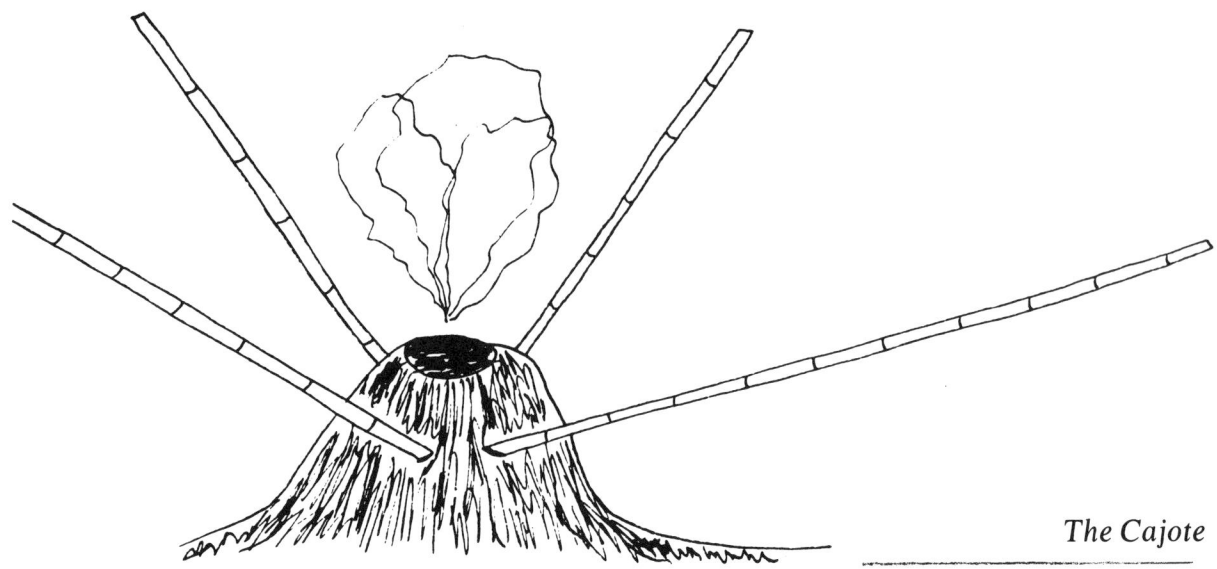

The Cajote

cajote, the pipe was passed from one to another in a circle—a modification of their earlier style but evidence that the friendly spirit of the *cajote* still endured.

In 1846, a visitor to Polynesia noted:

> *After the morning meal was concluded, pipes were lighted; and among them my own especial pipe, a present from the noble Mehevi. The islanders, who only smoke a whiff or two at a time, and at long intervals, and who keep their pipes going from hand to hand continually, regarded my systematic smoking of four or five pipefuls of tobacco in succession as something quite wonderful. When two or three pipes had circulated freely, the company gradually broke up.*
>
> —Herman Melville,
> Typee

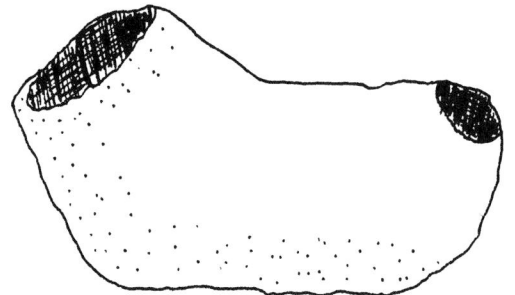

The Earthen Pipe

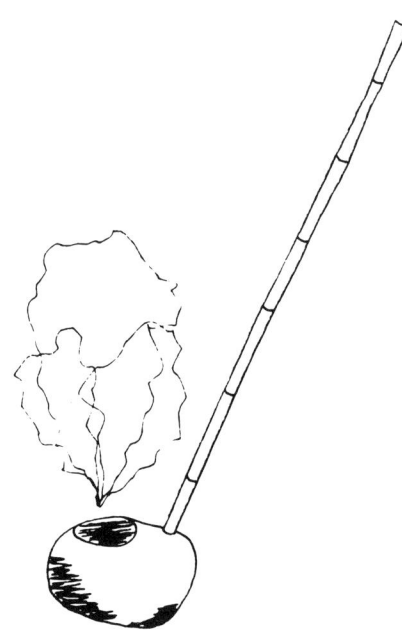

The Reed Pipe

The Cloud Blowers

In the forested islands of Canada one day, Jacques Cartier happened across a troop of Iroquois braves. At a standstill near a river, they were refreshing themselves after the hunt. Interested, Cartier approached the tranquil hunters, and observed this intriguing sight: Several of the Indians had pulled out "a hollow piece of stone or wood like a . . . cornet," packed it, laid "a coal of fire upon it . . . and proceeded to fill their bodies full of smoke." Intent on a cordial reception, Cartier and his party tried this exotic custom, as the Indians eagerly offered it. "We tried to use this smoke," Cartier recounts in his journals, "but on putting it to our mouths, it seemed hot as pepper." Cartier's account, entered in 1545, attests to the Canadian Indians' use of an unsophisticated device currently called *the straight or tube pipe.*

Possibly the oldest of all, the humble tube has been carbon-dated at about 2000 B.C. Popular in virtually every cranny of civilization, it is as versatile as Nature herself. In Russia, for instance, "the horn of beef" served, while in Africa the Hottentots carved theirs from the marrow bones of sheep. In other lands, pottery, root, antelope horn, serpentine, walrus tusk, and, in short, whatever the environment supplied was utilized. One tribe of coastal Indians, it is recorded, used "the short claw of a lobster," a tube that had a capacity of ten ordinary pipes.

In fact, before the debut of "clays," a sort of tube served the original London tobacconists, the sailors. "You will observe shipmasters and all others who come back from out there," noted one chap, "using little funnels, made of palm leaves or straws, in

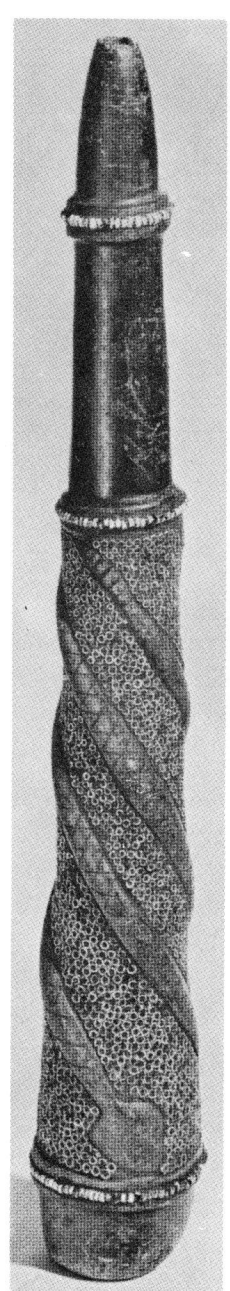

Cloud Blower with Three Serpents Twisted Around the Tube (Courtesy of the North Carolina Museum of Art. Pipe is in the collection of the Museum of the American Indian, Heye Foundation, New York)

17

The Earliest Illustration of a Tobacco Plant and the Operation of Smoking

the extreme end of which they stuff of this plant. This they light, and opening their mouths as much as they can, they suck in the smoke with their breath.'' If this sounds suspiciously like a crude cigar, it is because, ostensibly, the tube did evolve from it. A practical refinement, the tube offered a cool and tasty smoke in a durable wrapper.

Like the earliest level of earth smoking, nonetheless, the straight tube did have its imperfections. Due to its severe shape, the leaves had to be packed into the tube and then held in place by a stopper of sorts, usually a pebble. Another measure, that of lying on one's back, tilted the tube up to accommodate the smoker. Then, because the hot ashes could inadvertently be drawn into the mouth, the tube needed a screen, usually a plug of grass. This screen of grass actually had a triple function; not only did it trap ashes, but the foul juices of combustion as well. In addition, once the nicotine-soaked grass was removed from the tube and thoroughly dried, it could be smoked and frequently was.

ON KEEPING IT IN

What are the real evils and plagues of this age? What but its breathless fuss and brainless flutter, its bother and din and hurry-scurry, its glare and stare and pretension? Now, the pipe calms a man; it slackens his pulse, lulls his restlessness, lays unruly haste and anxiety to sleep, and makes a man willing to stay in the armchair and enjoy it as one of the pleasantest and most comfortable things in life, and let the world, if it will, go a-gadding. Your true smoker—he that keeps his pipe in, I mean; and that is the mark by which you may know the true from the sham smoker—your true smoker is a pattern man for consistency. He takes his time about things. You ask his opinion: he thinks twice before he answers once—keeping his pipe in. You offer him a bargain: he considers well before he accepts it—keeping his pipe in. Some ill-natured, quarrelsome fellow tries to provoke him; but he is slow to be provoked—he keeps his pipe in. He does not bore people to death, and usurp all the time for talking, in a company—he keeps his pipe in, and when he speaks, he does not tell all he knows, and exhaust all his wit, so as to have none left for the next holiday—he keeps his pipe in.

—Adam Hornbook
(Thomas Cooper)

A device commonplace to nearly all epochs, the tube pipe had a significant role in the civilizations of ancient Mexico. Used in both pleasurable and ceremonial activities, masterly wrought tubes of tortoiseshell and silver are not uncommon archeological finds. Wafer, in his *Travels* (1680), describes the custom of a certain Panamanian tribe, descendants of the ancient Mayans.

The dried tobacco leaves are stripped from the stalk, and laying two or three leaves one upon the other, they roll all up sideways into a long roll, yet leaving a little hollow; round this they roll other leaves one after another in the same manner, but close and hard, till the roll is as big as one's wrist and two or three feet in length. Their way of smoking when they are in company together is thus: A boy lights one end of a roll and burns it to a coal, wetting the part next to it to keep from wasting too fast; the end so lighted, he puts it into his mouth, and blows the smoke through the whole length of the roll into the face of everyone of the company or council, though there be two or three hundred of them. Then they, sitting in their usual posture upon forms, make with their hands held together a kind of funnel around their mouths and noses; into this they receive the smoke as it is blown upon them, snuffing it up greedily and strongly, as long as ever they are able to hold their breath, and seeming to bless themselves as it were with the refreshment it gives them.

This practice of blowing over a large assembly, once executed by a tube instead of a colossal cigar, is indigenous to Central

The Smoker of Palenque   (Illustration by Charles Fellows, reprinted from Weber's Guide to Pipes, Copyright 1962 by Cornerstone Library, Inc.)

America. Our source, dating back to about A.D. 400, is the celebrated Smoker of Palenque. A bas-relief found at a ruined temple in the province of Chiapas, southern Mexico, he is Tlaloc the Mayan rain god. From a tube held prayerlike in his hands, he is blowing clouds of smoke; hence the name, cloud blower.

These clouds of smoke, the Mayans divined, were closely connected to rain clouds. Consequently, the tube pipe assisted their priests in securing rain for the crops, their livelihood. In elaborate ceremony, they offered clouds of tobacco and incense smoke to the sun and to the four cardinal points. Gradually, as their shamanistic beliefs crumbled, smoking became a pleasurable pastime and the cloud blower an instrument of blissful satisfaction at gatherings such as previously described. Indeed, if we can trust the chroniclers of the Aztec conquest, it was a humble tube pipe that the Emperor Montezuma II smoked after his defeat at the hands of the Spanish.

How to Make a Tube Pipe

Although there are many possible materials that might be employed, I am convinced that wood, stone, or clay are the most eminently befitting, the latter of which must unfortunately be dispensed with as a conversant knowledge of the potter's art as well as a firing kiln would be necessary. The remaining materials, however, offer excellent possibilities: They are easy to work with, are durable, and provide a cool and fragrant smoke, plus the work can be accomplished with only a few tools.

Mandatory for all pipe making is the drill, preferably an electrically powered one and an assortment of wood and masonry bits. Other tools, such as saws and files, can be purchased inexpensively at any hardware store. Also, a good vise—the type that clamps to your workbench—is very handy.

To make a wooden tube, you first need to select an appropriate wood. Pine and spruce, for instance, are too soft for this sort of pipe and are likely to burn out after a while. On the other hand, cherry, teak, rosewood, and other hardwoods will not. These close-grained woods are surprisingly heat resistant and will provide many years of tasty smokes. Seasoned hardwoods can be procured from a large number of reputable merchants, though Albert Constantine (2050 Eastchester Road, Bronx, New York, 10461) has a mail-order service.

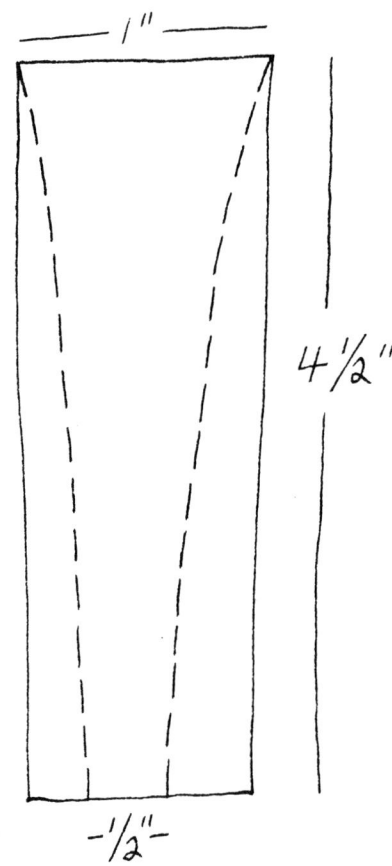

Figure 1

You will need a piece about one-inch wide by one-inch deep by four and a half inches long. Clamp it in your vise and make cuts as indicated in Figure 1, noting that while most hardwoods will cut with an ordinary saw, for

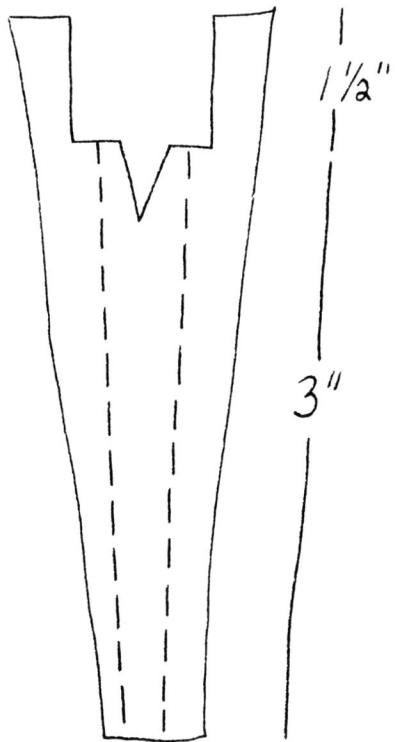

Figure 2

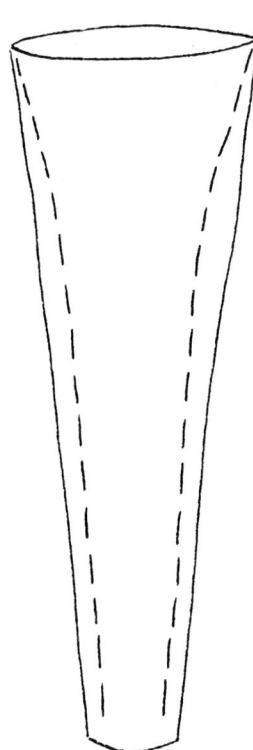

Figure 3

some you will have to use a hacksaw. As the cuts should be as accurate as possible, score off the cut lines before sawing.

Next, chuck a three-quarter-inch wood-boring bit into your drill and drill as indicated in Figure 2, making certain that the depth of the hole does not exceed one and one half inches. Too large a bowl does not season properly, and this can lead to damage. Then, chuck a one-quarter-inch twist drill into your drill and proceed to bore the smoke hole as in Figure 2. Do this slowly, being cautious that the hole should be true and straight. When this is completed, there will be a circular ledge at the junction of the "bowl" and "stem." Here a three-quarter-inch screen (standard size in most "head" shops) will rest. The pipe is now rough-finished.

To complete, use coarse sandpaper and contour the tube as indicated in Figure 3. Gradually, work your way down to extra-fine grit and smooth the surface. In the final sanding, remember to sand with the grain of the wood only, as rubbing against the grain will leave scratch marks. At the same time, smooth the interior of the tube the same way, twisting a piece of sandpaper around a thin (eighth-inch) dowel to get into the smoke hole. Finally, to produce a really nice luster, rub a little carnauba wax into the wood and polish the tube with a soft cloth.

To make a stone tube, you'd best use one of the softer varieties such as soap-, sand-, or limestone. Other stones such as marble and even granite may also be used, though these harder varieties are not worked so easily.

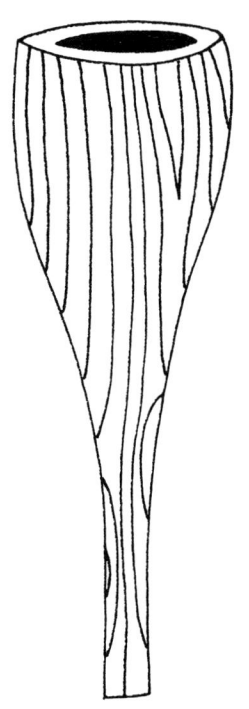

Figure 4

Basically the process is the same as for the wood, but a hacksaw and masonry bits will be needed. Once the pipe has been rough-finished, use a half-round file to contour the outside and a six-inch round file (rattail) for the inside. To make the surface smooth, use emery cloth followed by steel wool. Then, if you'd like the stone to really shine, apply a little hot beeswax to it and rub it smartly. With long use, however, the stone will take on a handsome lustrous look naturally.

How to Smoke a Tube Pipe

Used extensively in India, Pakistan, Afghanistan etc., the tube pipe (or *chillum* as it is called there) yields an extraordinary smoke, provided it is smoked properly.

Above all, the tube should never touch the lips; this is one of the chillum's principal attractions in countries in which sanitary conditions make such a pipe a real blessing. By smoking it in the fashion illustrated below, the pipe may be both freely circulated without fear of contagion and smoked to its best advantage. Sometimes a *sofi* cloth is used; basically a wet scrap of fabric that is wound around the *chillum* to keep it cool after heavy smoking, it is often embroidered with prayers and symbols that honor the edifying herbs therein.

The prototype of all pipes, the plain tube has several interesting derivatives. On the islands of the South Pacific, where the bamboo plant thrives, the natives use a *baubau* with staggering results. Usually about eighteen inches in length and an inch and a half in diameter, a cylinder of bamboo is perforated with a small hole at either end. In one hole, a leaf filled with the smoking mixture is fitted (recently hand-rolled like a cigarette). The smoker then places his lips over the other hole, the mixture is lighted, and smoke is drawn into the cylinder. This is repeated until the mixture is depleted and the baubau fairly brimming with smoke. No smoke is as yet inhaled, and usually a woman will thus "charge it" for the men. Once filled, the tube is passed from one to another, each smoker taking deep pulls of the dense smoke.

Lewis[*] reports:

The effects of this kind of smoking appear to be very severe. The men always seem quite dazed for a second or two or even longer after a single inhala-

22

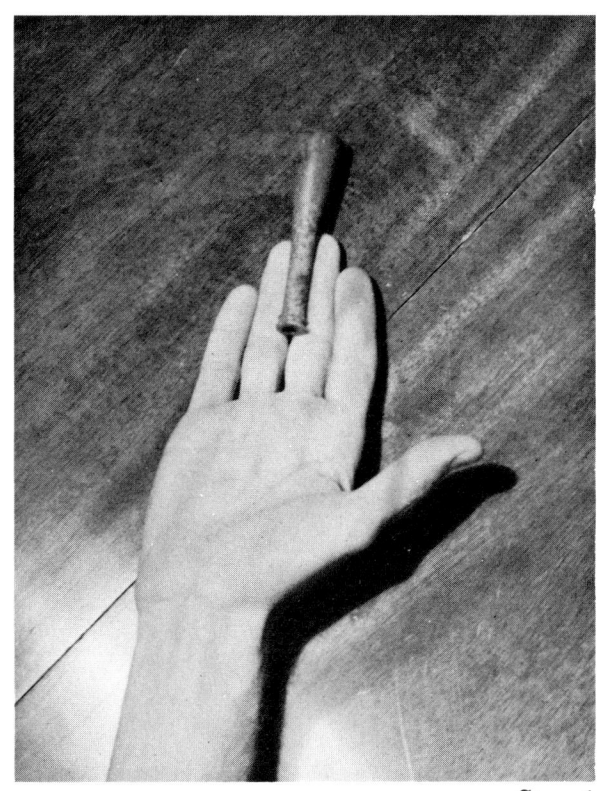
Step 1

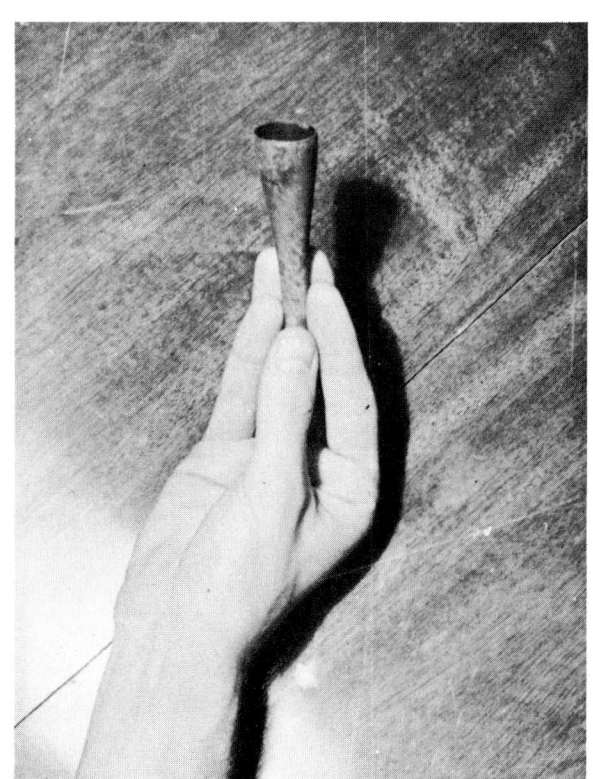
Step 2

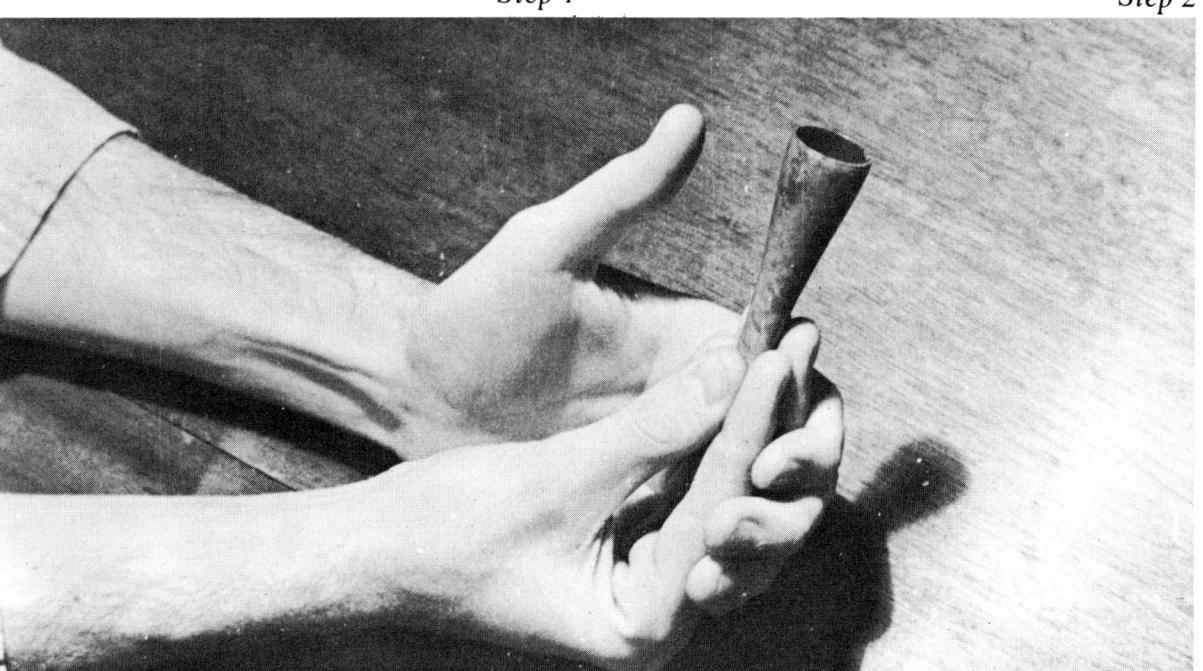
Step 3

23

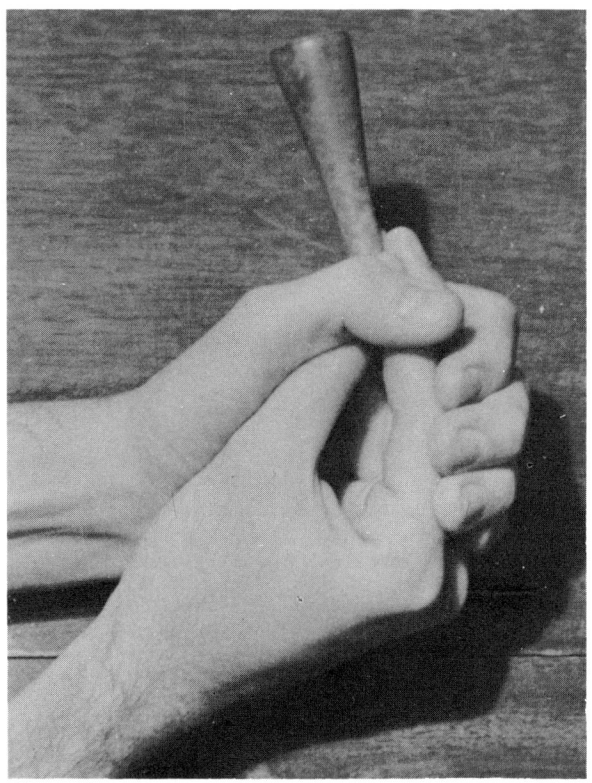
Step 4

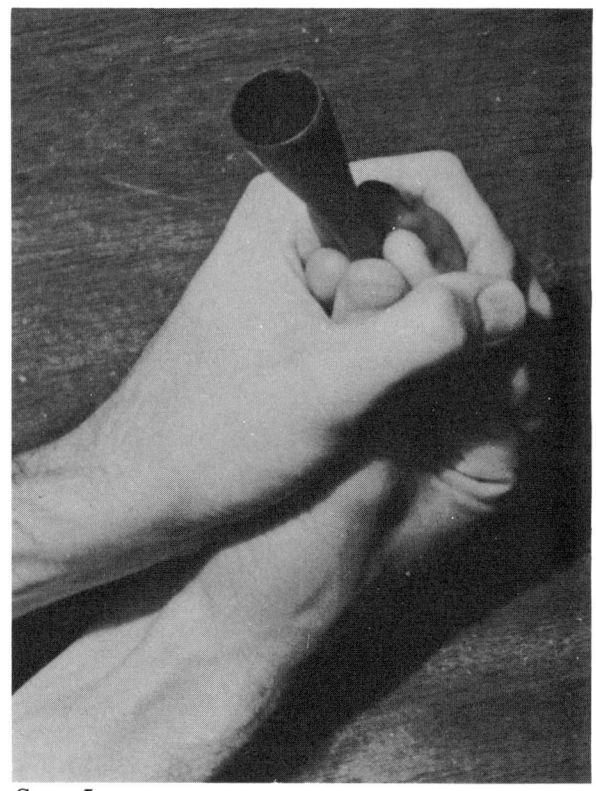
Step 5

Step 6

tion, but they enjoy it greatly and prize tobacco highly. I have seen an old man reel and stagger from the effects of one pull at the pipe . . . I have seen a native so affected by a single inhalation as to be rendered senseless.

With this to recommend it, the *baubau* ought to be an essential part of every smoker's arsenal, for what the cask does for wine the *baubau* does for smoke, rendering it potent yet mellow. Delightful for tobacco, the *baubau* is perfect for *Cannabis*.

*Albert B. Lewis, "Use of Tobacco in New Guinea and Neighboring Regions," Field Museum of Natural History, Leaflet 17 (1924).

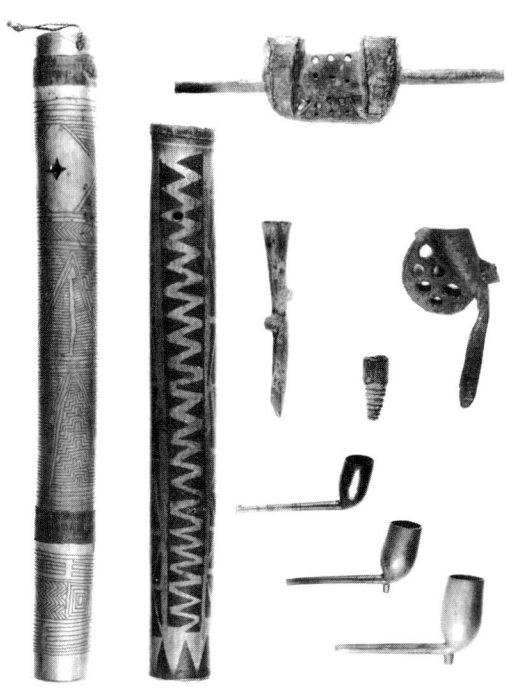

A Collection of Pipes from the South Seas, Including Two Baubaus, Three Trade Pipes, Two Tube Pipes, One Unusual Double Pipe, and a Free-Form Pipe.   (Courtesy of the Field Museum of Natural History, Chicago)

Three Smiling Baubau Smokers (Courtesy of the Field Museum of Natural History, Chicago)

In the photographs of the native *baubau* smokers, you will see two possibilities: the smoke hole at the end of the tube and the smoke hole on the side. The tobacco hole never varies. Personally, I prefer the side as it is easier on the lips, being more shapely than flat. To perforate the cylinder, you can use either a drill or a wood-burning iron. If you use the drill, a one quarter inch bit for the smoke hole and either a seven thirty-second inch or a three sixteenth inch bit for the tobacco hole are nicely accomodating. With the iron, of course, you must approximate these diameters.

How to Make a Baubau

To make the baubau is simple once a suitable piece of bamboo has been obtained. It must be a complete cell (that is, cut beyond the natural divisions of the stalk so that it is completely air-tight). It should be approximately eighteen inches long and an inch and a half in diameter though these dimensions may vary according to individual taste or what's available.

How to Smoke a Baubau

Although a twisted leaf serves as an efficient wrapper, cigarette rolling papers are swiftly renovating the baubau industry. First of all, they are especially made to burn with a bare minimum of taste and harshness and, secondly, are considerably easier to handle. The photographs below illustrate how to create a perfect conical encasement. Remember not to wet the gummed edges but sparingly.

Step 1

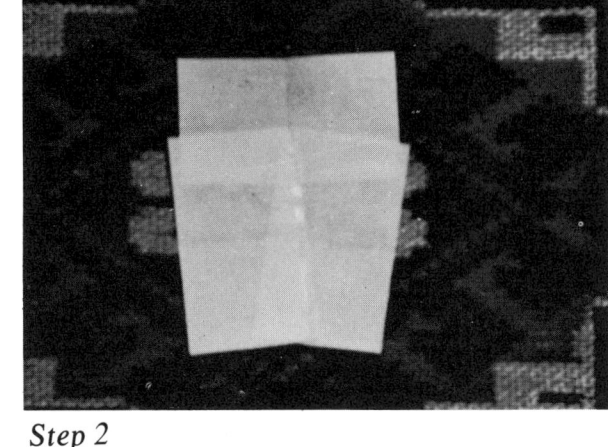

Step 2

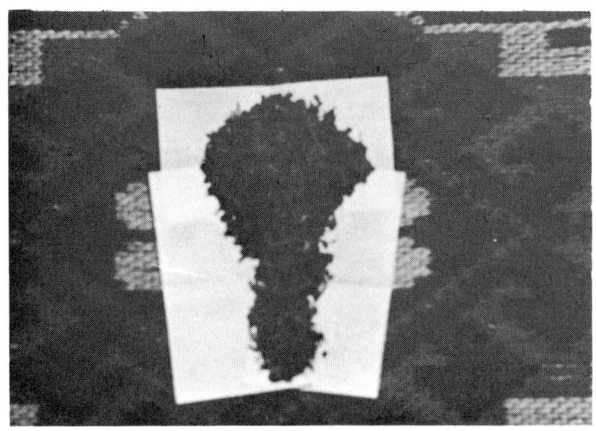

Step 3

Step 4

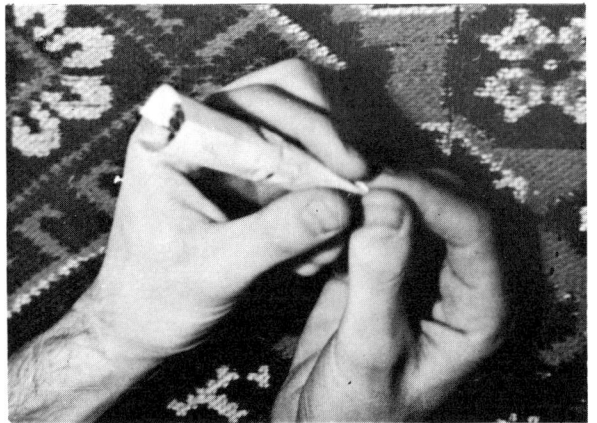

Step 5

Step 6

Step 7 (Ready for Smoking)

South Sea Native Smoking the Baubau on His Front Porch   (Courtesy of the Field Museum of Natural History, Chicago)

To smoke the baubau, first set the cone in the tobacco hole with a slight twisting motion. Then have a friend or servant hold a match over it while you suck in easily at the smoke hole. Try to avoid inhaling just yet; rather, draw the smoke into your mouth and return it to the tube with a gentle in and out rhythm. Keep it up until the cone is depleted and the *baubau* fully charged. To smoke, or rather inhale, lightly press your thumb over the tobacco hole so that it is now very nearly sealed off, but not quite. You will find that a touch of air must be admitted with each inhalation. Learn to regulate the air/smoke mixture to suit your taste, and you will enjoy an incomparably mellifluous smoke.

Eskimo Pipes

Pipe smoking had already circled the globe before it reached Alaska. Its sturdy inhabitants, the Eskimos, were nearly entirely dependent on the sea for food, clothing, tools, and solace from the bleak arctic wasteland. It was only natural, therefore, that their pipes, too, should have been foraged from the sea. Hence, in the seventeenth century, after their neighbors across the Bering Strait—the Chukches—introduced them to the pleasures of pipe smoking, they found in the walrus's tusk a natural pipe.

Characteristic of these pipes is a separate bowl, usually carved of tusk, though metal ones are not uncommon. The stems are elaborately decorated, often with scenes depicting their constant search for food. Returning from the hunt, a whale and several seals their prize, is the scene on the larger pipe. On the other, a man is depicted harpooning some four-legged creature while birds flutter about.

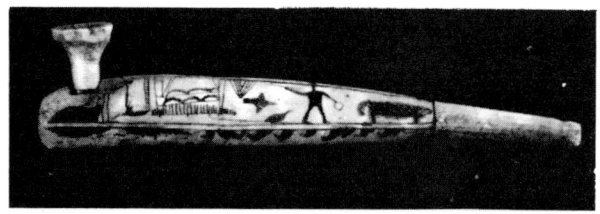
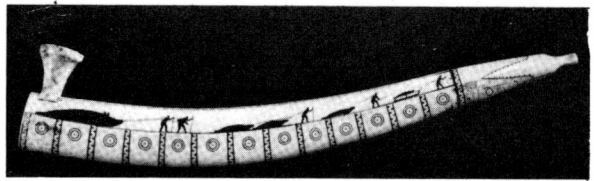

Two Eskimo Pipes of Walrus Tusk (Property of the Public Museum of Milwaukee)

THE SECRET, AWFUL VICE

I am not, in the first place, what is called a ladies' man, having contracted an irrepressible habit of smoking after dinner, which has obliged me to give up a great deal of the dear creatures' society; nor can I go to country-houses for the same reason. Say what they will, ladies do not like you to smoke in their bed-rooms; their silly little noses scent out the odor upon the chintz, weeks after you have left them . . . What is this smoking that it should be considered a crime? I believe in my heart that women are jealous of it, as of a rival. They speak of it as some secret, awful vice that seizes upon a man, and makes him a Pariah from genteel society. I would lay a guinea that many a lady who has just been kind enough to read the above lines, lays down the book, after this confession of mine that I am a smoker, and says, "Oh, that vulgar wretch!" and passes on to something else.

—William Thackeray
  The Confessions of Fitz-Boodle

INDIANS OF THE VALLEYS AND PLAINS

Mound Pipes

Where the Canadian flatlands stretch into the northern reaches of the United States, a chain of lakes—the Great Lakes—lies. There, undisturbed for centuries, lived the tribes Cree, Arapaho, Chippewa, Shawnee, Ojibway, and others; together these related Indian tribes formed an extensive and prosperous nation, the great Algonquin. Green and dark forests, the Lakes and countless rivulets all provided an abundance of life's necessities. Then, still long before the Discovery, pugnacious neighbors to the north descended upon them and drove them from their homeland.

Down the Ohio and Mississippi rivers they fled, leaving their land but keeping their traditions. A superstitious people, they believed fervently in a life hereafter; subsequently, whenever members of the nation died, their possessions were placed beside them in the grave. Like the ancient Egyptians, they built monuments to the dead on the order of huge burial vaults above ground. A considerably simpler people, the Algonquins could not match the grandeur of the pyramids of the Nile but instead constructed earth mounds in which the dead and their possessions slept. Recently (nineteenth and twentieth centuries), these mounds have been excavated, and the unearthings have thrown much light on the culture of these people.

The scattered tribes migrated slowly south as the fierce tribes of the north extended their rule. Consequently, the oldest Algonquin mounds can be found in the north, specifically in Ohio. Located here is the famous "Mound City," a telling cache of artifacts from centuries past. Considered as some of

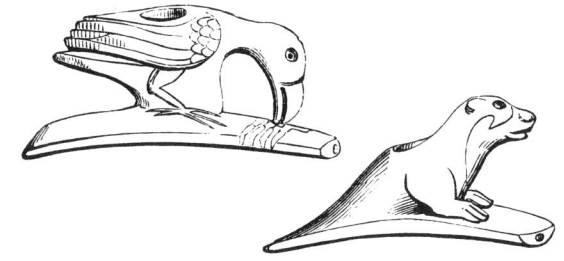

the more revealing objects are over two hundred stone pipes; highly stylized, these pipes exhibit at least one important aspect of Algonquin civilization.

These ancient pipes, coupled with today's archeological techniques, confirm that the Algonquins practiced a form of totem worship as did many other primitive nations; that is, each tribe or clan or even household held one particular creature as a cognate spirit, a true spiritual brother. Thus, the chosen creature was venerated as befits a deity. Some tribes, for instance, carved elaborate totem poles on which these creatures stood guard over councils and lodges. The Algonquins, being of the persuasion that tobacco was a sacred herb and consuming it a sacred act, carved their creatures into the design of their pipes, the happy result being that some of these stone artifacts are among the most graceful and fanciful objects ever unearthed.

Of course, wooden totem pipes once existed, but due to the forces of erosion, none remain.

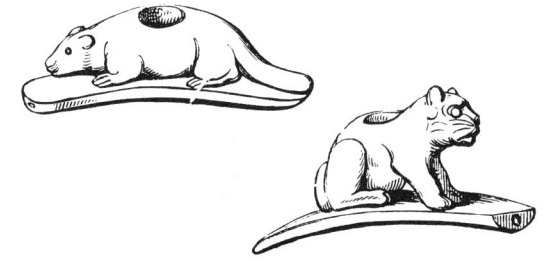

Four Totem Pipes Excavated from Algonquin Mounds

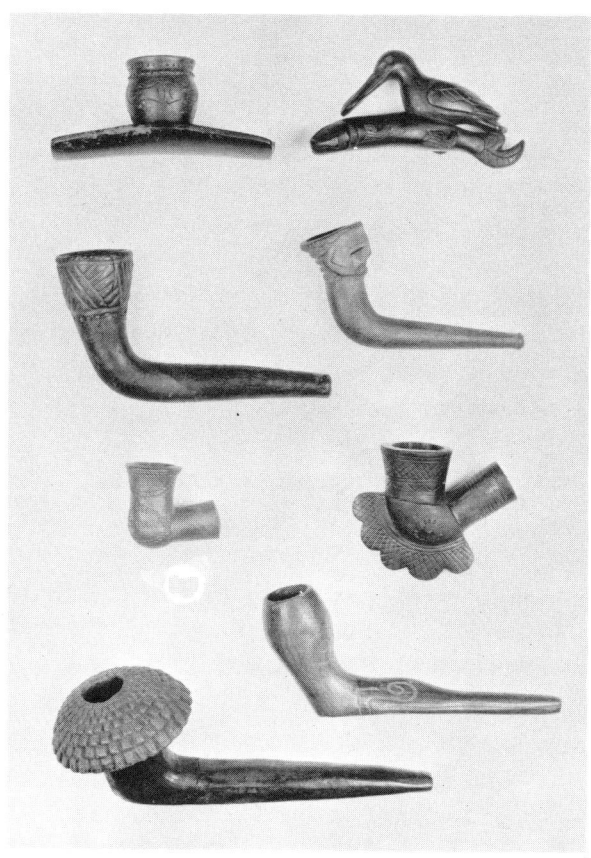

An Assortment of Aboriginal American Smoking Pipes   (Courtesy of the Field Museum of Natural History, Chicago)

The characteristic shape of these pipes is a flat, slightly curved base—of which one end serves as a stem, the other a handle. Atop it sits the bowl, carved artistically like some creature and nearly centered. The creatures are all alike in respect that all of them face the smoker but are of so vast a variety as to make one curious about the faunal constitution of this area of North America. In addition to the toad, lizard, bear, bird, and other commonplace critters, the elephant and the sea cow have turned up on these pipes. The elephant is indigenous to India and Africa, and no elephants trod the vales of Ohio; likewise, the sea cow haunts the tropical climes and is never seen north of the Gulf of Mexico. How, then, do these creatures come to decorate the artifacts found in Ohio? Evidently, travelers from distant lands visited the Algonquins and related descriptions of these exotic beasts to them. In turn, the Indians must have reasoned that such puissant creatures had intimate connections with puissant deities and so elected to venerate them. This theory raises some intriguing questions concerning the earliest exploration of the continent by outsiders.

Because their exodus led them south, the Algonquins eventually touched the periphery of the southeastern Indian nation. Learning mound building from their new neighbors, these Creeks, Chickasaws, Seminoles, and other tribes of the Southeast buried, too, a goodly assortment of their possessions, pipes included. These pipes are of special interest: The bowls have been shifted to one end and tilt away from the smoker, and though some of them are complete unto themselves, others require a reed or hollow shoot to serve for the stem. It was from these Indians especially that the early (fifteenth-century) explorers learned to use tobacco. Consequently, when European pipe makers looked for patterns to emulate, they chose those of their teachers. In this fashion, the indomitable "clay" was born.

I have no doubt that it is from the habit of smoking that . . . the American Indians are such monstrous well-bred men. The pipe draws wisdom from the lips of the philosopher, and shuts up the mouth of the foolish: it generates a style of conversation, contemplative, thoughtful, benevolent, and unaffected . . . May I die if I

abuse that kindly weed which has given me so much pleasure!
—*William Thackeray*
Sketches and Travels

Calumet: the Pipe of Peace

Perhaps no other nation recorded in the annals of civilization has devotedly held such reverence for tobacco and smoking pipes as the Indians of the Plains. Accordingly, there are scores of myths that contribute to the tradition of the obscure origin of the weed. One of them, a representative of all such tales, goes like this: One day long ago, a heavenly voice suddenly spoke. All the people, the voice admonished, should stay indoors, for a boat carrying medicine men would soon be on the river; those that observed its passing would be struck dead instantly and mercilessly. The boat did pass, and the nonbelievers died. Later on, the people looked for the boat and found it ashore, upriver. Instead of medicine men, however, the vessel held two alien beings, both fast asleep. Once again, the heavenly voice spoke: "Put these beings to death," it said, "and a great blessing shall you receive." And so the people did as the voice instructed and buried their victims' ashes. Days later, several plants shot up from the earth where the ashes were buried, and thus the promised blessing—tobacco—was bestowed. Understandably, because of the Indian nation's vast diversification, the content of each tale differs; the theme, on the other hand, never does. Tobacco, all Indian lore contends, is a heavenly blessing.

Tobacco, the Indians insisted, could convey deific capabilities to mere mortals. Gods, for instance, need not eat or drink, and, by using tobacco, neither did men. To stave off hunger and thirst, the Indians first burned certain river or sea shells and then ground them into a powder. They next added this powder to an equal amount of tobacco and chewed the blend until it became a solid lump. Little pills of the stuff were then shaped and left to dry in the sun. On trips or retreats, a few of these tablets—set to dissolve naturally under the tongue—staved off hunger and thirst for four, five, and even six days. It was as the administrator of such wonderful boons as this that tobacco became a treasured possession and a savory companion.

It was not this aspect, nonetheless, that advocated the intense respect the Indians had for tobacco. In its ascent to the heavens—as tobacco smoke rose in clouds from their pipes—they believed that it carried their fondest hopes and most heartfelt prayers to the ears of their gods, they themselves residents of heaven. Convinced that the smoke was a viable thoroughfare to the celestial throne, Indians put not only tobacco in their pipes but, symbolically at least, the entire universe. The following, coming from the Oglala Sioux's ceremony called "Releasing the Soul," is the rite that occurs upon the death of a tribesman and demonstrates the nature of their reverence for tobacco.

The helper of the keeper of the soul then takes a pipe, and holding it up to the heavens, he cries: "Behold, O Wa-kan-Tanka! We are now about to do Thy will. With all the sacred beings of the universe, we offer to You this pipe!"

The helper then takes a pinch of the

sacred tobacco *kinnikinnik*, and holding it and the stem of the pipe toward the west, he cries: "With this *wakan* tobacco, we place You in the pipe, O winged Power of the west. We are about to send our voices to *Wakan-Tanka*, and we wish You to help us!

This day is *wakan* because a soul is to be released. All over the universe there will be happiness and rejoicing! O You sacred Power of the place where the sun goes down, it is a great thing we are doing in placing You in the pipe. Give to us for our rites one of the two sacred red and blue days which you control!"

This Power of the west, now in the tobacco, is placed in the pipe, and holding another pinch of *kinnikinnik* towards the north, the helper prays.

"O You, Thunder-being, there where *Waziah* has his lodge, who comes with the purifying winds, and who guards the health of the people; O Bald-headed Eagle of the north, Your wings never tire! There is a place for you too in this pipe, which will be offered to *Wakan-Tanka*. Help us, and give to us one of Your two sacred days."

Then holding another pinch of *kinnikinnik* to the east, the helper continues to pray.

"O You sacred Being of the place where the sun comes up, who controls knowledge! Yours is the path of the rising sun which brings light into the world. Your name is *Huntka*, for You have wisdom and are long-winged. There is a place for You in the pipe; help us in sending our voice to *Wakan-Tanka!* Give to us Your sacred days!"

This Power of the east is placed in the pipe, and then another pinch of *kinnikinnik* is held toward the south, with the prayer: "O You who guard that path leading to the place towards which we always face, and upon which our generations walk, we are placing You in this sacred pipe! You control our life, and the lives of all the people of the universe. Everything that moves and all that is will send a voice to *Wakan-Tanka*. We have a place for You in the pipe; help us in sending our voice, and give to us one of Your good days! This we ask of You, O White Swan, there where we always face."

The stem of the pipe and a pinch of *kinnikinnik* are then held towards the earth.

"O You, sacred Earth, from whence we have come, You are humble, nourishing all things; we know that You are *wakan* and that with You we are all as relatives. Grandmother and Mother Earth who bear bruit, for You there is a place in this pipe. O Mother, may Your people walk the path of life, facing the strong winds! May we walk firmly upon You! May our steps not falter! We and all who move upon You are sending our voices to *Wakan-Tanka!* Help us! All together as one we cry: help us!"

"When the pipe has thus been filled with all the Powers and with all that there is in the universe, it is given to the keeper of the soul, who takes it and, crying as he walks, goes to the tipi of the keeper of the most sacred pipe . . . Entering the tipi, and holding out the pipe with its stem pointing toward the south, he places it in the hands of the keeper of the pipe."*

*From *The Sacred Pipe: Black Elk's Account of the Seven Rites of the Oglala Sioux*, by Joseph Epes Brown. Copyright 1953 by the University of Oklahoma Press.

In this manner, the pipe contains all that there is in the universe—its sole function to entreat the Great and All-Powerful Spirit, *Wakan-Tanka*, to bestow favors, vision, and inspiration.

Contrary to popular belief, Indians did not use *Cannabis* or its derivatives; rather, they smoked a distinctive blend of tobacco and other selected leaves and bark commonly called *kinnikinnik*. This they loved dearly and carried it about in doeskin pouches. It is a natural product and offers the smoker the serenity of Nature, a scent of fields and forest and a taste of heaven.

How to Make Kinnikinnik (Indian Tobacco)

To make an ounce of *kinnikinnik*, you ought to use a very mild tobacco. Virginia and burley are perhaps the best, though some might prefer the sweeter cavandish. But the stronger tobaccos such as perique, latakia, and the Turkish leaves should be avoided. Put about one-third of an ounce of tobacco in a wooden or ceramic bowl.

The second ingredient is dried sumac leaves, of which one-third of an ounce is also required. To dry the leaves, either set them in the sun or a slow oven, but if you use an oven, be sure not to crisp them. Crumple the leaves with your hands and add them to the tobacco.

Thirdly, you will need the inner bark of either a willow or dogwood tree. Peel off the tough outer bark first; the inner bark will be almost velvety and slightly damp. Peel the inner bark into long thin strips and allow them to dry as previously described. Then pulverize the bark by rubbing it briskly between your hands, reducing it to a powder if you can. Sprinkle it into the tobacco and sumac-leaves mixture.

The most thorough method of mixing the ingredients is to put them all in a large plastic bag, twist shut the top, and shake vigorously. A few drops of vegetable or safflower oil might be added to settle the dust. This, then, is the basic *kinnikinnik* recipe. Some tribes, according to their location, supplemented this recipe with other ingredients. The California tribes, for instance, used to crush abalone shells and add them to their *kinnikinnik*, which, as reports have it, caused them to be exceedingly drunk after smoking. More conventional additives were columbine seeds, the intoxicating Jamestown weed, and for flavor the musk of the rat by that name.

Gitche Manito, the mighty,
The creator of the nations,
Looked upon them with compassion,
With paternal love and pity;
Looked upon their wrath and wrangling
But as quarrels among children,
But as feuds and fights of children! . . .
"I am weary of your quarrels,
Weary of your wars and bloodshed,
Weary of your prayers for
vengeance . . .
Bathe now in the stream before you,
Wash the war-paint from your faces,

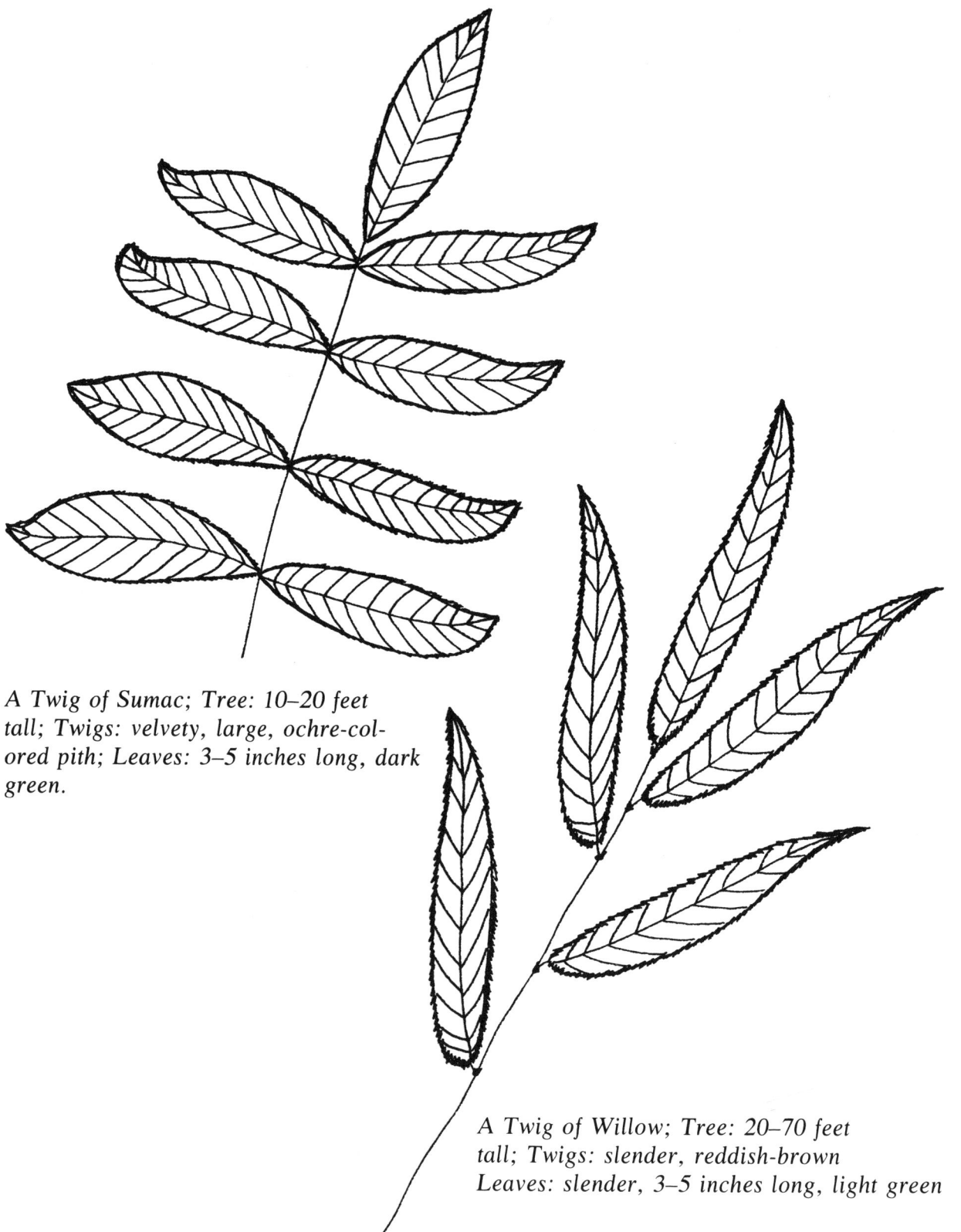

A Twig of Sumac; Tree: 10–20 feet tall; Twigs: velvety, large, ochre-colored pith; Leaves: 3–5 inches long, dark green.

A Twig of Willow; Tree: 20–70 feet tall; Twigs: slender, reddish-brown Leaves: slender, 3–5 inches long, light green

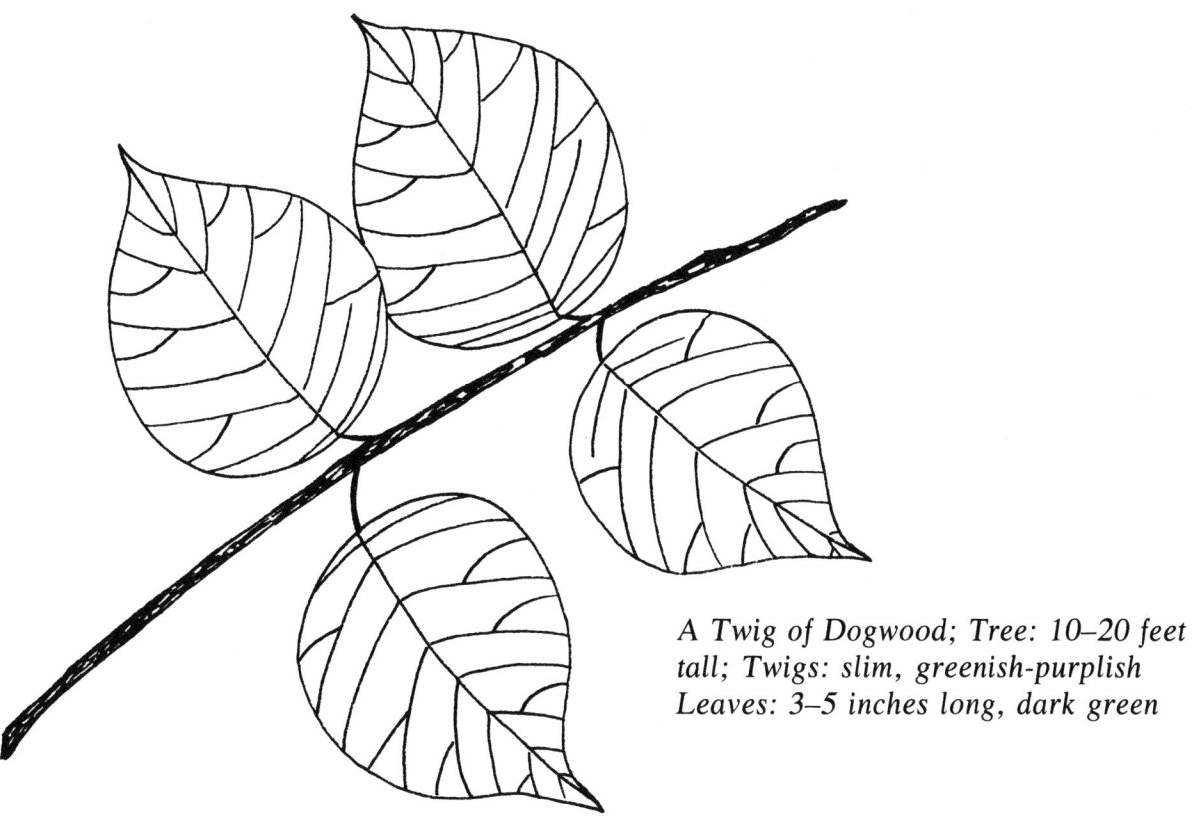

A Twig of Dogwood; Tree: 10–20 feet tall; Twigs: slim, greenish-purplish Leaves: 3–5 inches long, dark green

*Wash the blood-stains from your fingers,
Bury your war-clubs and your weapons,
Break the red stone from this quarry,
Mould and make it into Peace-Pipes,
Take the reeds that grow beside you,
Deck them with your brightest feathers,
Smoke the calumet together,
And as brothers live henceforward!"*
—Henry W. Longfellow
The Song of Hiawatha

The story of Catlinite—"the red stone"—is as old as Noah. When the catastrophic Flood occurred, the red people of all tribes convened on the *Coteau des Prairies*—a plateau in Minnesota. Ultimately, the *Coteau* submerged, and the people perished; the Great Spirit, however, caused their bodies to be changed into stone—red stone—and so created the Sacred Quarry. The flesh of their ancestors, the quarry belongs to all Indians, and the stone from this quarry they call pipestone.

In the 1830s, the artist George Catlin set out to live among the Sioux Indians to celebrate their colorful existence in oil paints. In addition to many memorable paintings, he recorded his observations in letters and journals.

He retells the Sioux legend:

Many ages after the red men were made, when all the different tribes were at war, the Great Spirit sent runners and called them all together at the "Red Pipe." He stood on the tops of the rocks, and the red people were assembled in infinite numbers on the plains below. He took out of the rock a piece of the red stone, and made a large pipe; he smoked it over them all; told them it was part of their flesh; that though they were at war, they must meet at this place as friends; that it belonged to them all; that they must make their calumets from it and smoke them to him whenever they wished to appease him or get his good-will—the smoke from his big pipe rolled over them all, and he disappeared in its cloud.

Subsequently, any red Indian who wanted to chisel a stone pipe had to travel to the Sacred Quarry. Some of the stories concerning the distances that Indians traveled to reach the "Red Pipe" are quite extraordinary: tales of lone braves traveling weeks transporting hundreds of pounds of pipestone are common.

Catlin, too, has the distinction of being the first white man ever to see the Sacred Quarry. Due to this fact, plus his immense contribution to the white man's understanding of the Indian experience, the red pipestone is today called Catlinite.

*   *

The word *calumet* is not Indian but Old French for "reed." Indeed, its conventional design seems—like a reed—rather unspectacular, but its appearance belies its true significance. For of all things in nature and art, none were so venerated as the calumet. An acknowledged token of peace, it enabled its bearer to pass untouched through territories ruled by hostile tribes; a covenant never violated. Foreigners particularly were astounded by this property of the pipe, many of whose lives were spared due to the timely appearance of one. "I had certainly perished in my voyage," avowed one English traveler, "had it not been for this Calumet or Pipe."

Besides assuring free and unobstructed travel, the calumet was smoked on all occasions that advanced a mutual trust or treaty. An eminent example of this occurred in 1795 at the ratification of the Treaty of Greenville, Ohio. There General "Mad Anthony" Wayne smoked the calumet with the chiefs of nearly one hundred tribes to seal the cession of the Northwest Territory. Occasionally, as a gesture of further credence, the chiefs of each tribe exchanged calumets; and to decline the offered pipe was regarded as a sign of blatant hostility, and the calumet would then be considered the Pipe of War.

But despite its paramount role as social mediator, the calumet's loftiest significance was in its spiritual guise: the pipe as universe.

Joseph Brown writes:

In filling the pipe, all space (represented by the offerings to the powers of the six directions) and all things (represented by the grains of tobacco) are contracted within a single point (the bowl or heart of the pipe), so that the pipe contains, or really *is*, the universe. But since the pipe is the universe, it is also man, and the one who fills a pipe should identify himself with it, thus not only establishing the center of the universe, but also his own center; he so "ex-

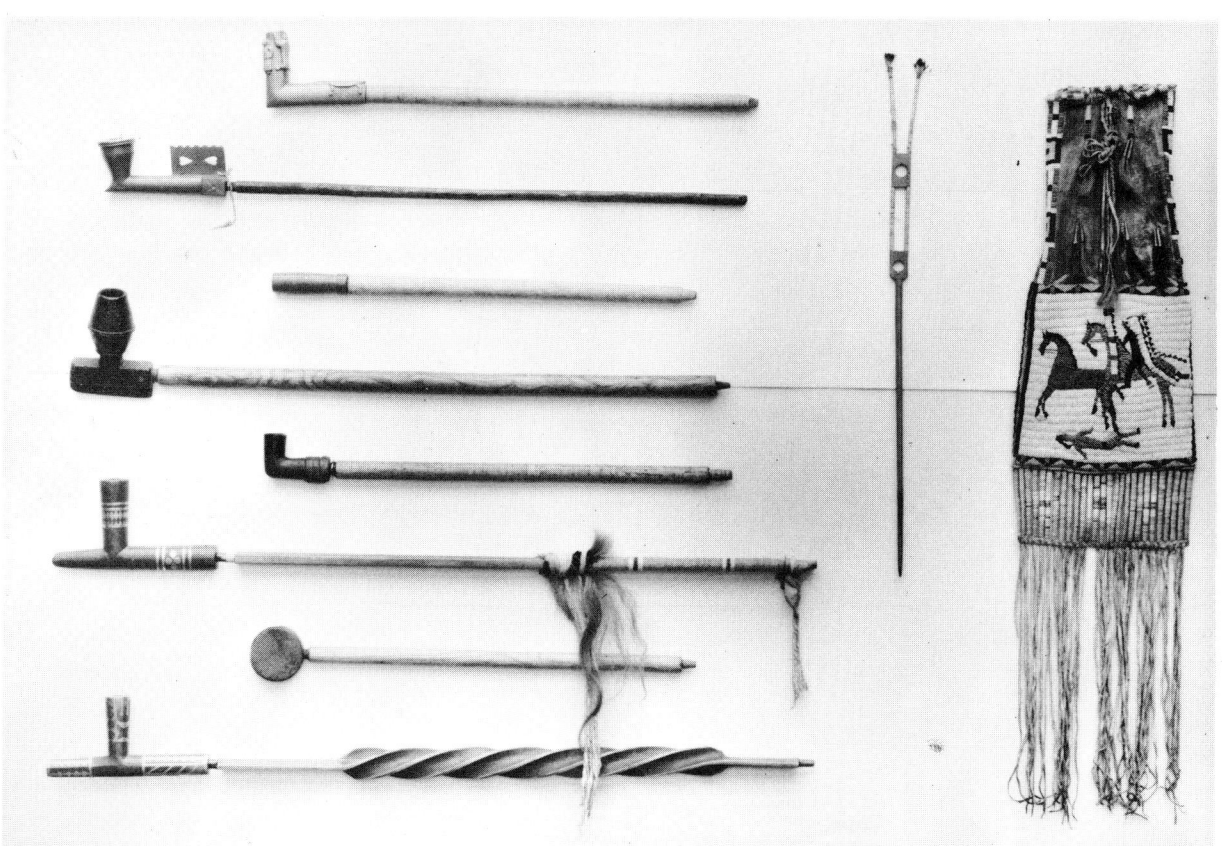

Pipes of the Plains' Indians and a Decorated Tobacco Pouch   (Courtesy of the Field Museum of Natural History, Chicago)

pands" that the six directions of space are actually brought within himself. It is by this expansion that a man ceases to be a part, a fragment, and becomes whole or holy; he shatters the illusion of separateness.

In order to make clear this identity for the Indian of the body of man with the pipe, [he quotes] the following text of the Osage Indians:

These people had a pipe,
Which they made to be their body.

O Hon-ga, I have a pipe that I have made to be my body;
If you also make it to be your body,
You shall have a body that is free from all causes of death.

Behold the joint of the neck, they said,
That I have made to be the joint of my own neck.

Behold the mouth of the pipe,
That I have made to be my mouth.

Behold the right side of the pipe,
That I have made to be the right side of my body.

Behold the spine of the pipe,
That I have made to be my own spine.

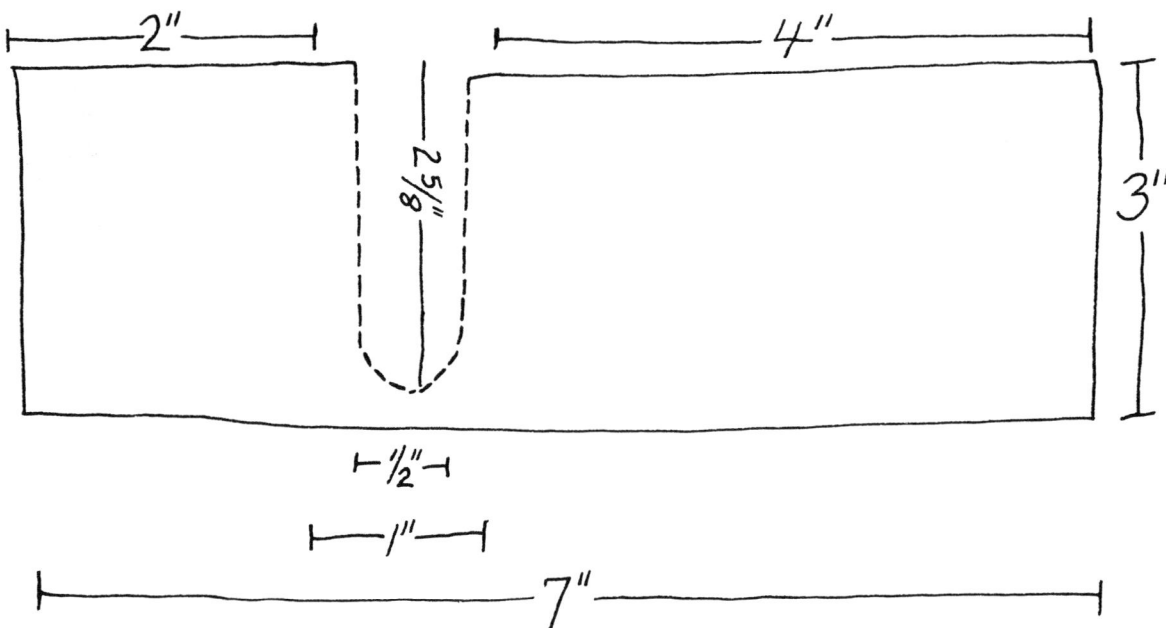

Figure 1

**Behold the left side of the pipe,
That I have made to be the left side of my own body.**

**Behold the hollow of the pipe,
That I have made to be the hollow of my own body.**

**Behold the thong that holds together the pipe and stem;
That I have made to be my windpipe.
. . . . use the pipe as an offering in your supplications,
Your prayers shall be readily granted.***

*From *The Sacred Pipe: Black Elk's Account of the Seven Rites of the Oglala Sioux*, by Joseph Epes Brown. Copyright 1953 by the University of Oklahoma Press.

This concept of pipe ♦ universe ♦ man was the quintessence of Indian spiritualism; not only did it bestow a deep-seated sense of integration to the individual, it fostered a natural sense of communal harmony for which the Indians are rightly famous.

Because spiritualism pervaded all facets of their lives, the pipe was never cold for long. The Oglalas, for example, used to conduct their lyrical Seven Rites in unison with the readying and smoking of pipes. Among these were the *Inipi* (Rite of Purification) and the *Wiwanyag Wachipi* (Sun Dance) as well as the *Hunkapi* (Making of Relatives) and the *Ishna Ta Awi Cha Lowan* (Preparing a Girl for Womanhood).

For these and other rites in which the Great Spirit's presence or benefaction was begged, the pipe was decorated. Some of the traditional decorations include eagle, owl, duck and woodpecker feathers (the deities of the day, night, water and trees respectively) and paint (blue to symbolize the sky, green the earth and red the pathway of the spirits); horsehair, porcupine quills, rabbit and beaver fur and even the heads of small birds have also been known to adorn these ceremonial pipes. But besides feathers and other such finery, dances and chants befitting the occasion helped to create an appropriately ritualistic mood. Indeed, the famous *Dance of the Calumet*, as Father Marquette noted in his *New Discovery of A Vast Country in America* (1698), "is a solemn Ceremony amongst the savages . . . performed in Winter-time in their Cabins, and in the open Field in the Summer." All in all, it helped to enhance the pipe's already hallowed status.

"The most mysterious thing in the world," declared Father Marquette, "the Sceptres of our Kings are not so much respected [as the calumet]." Certainly there is mystery in the calumet: it has accumulated in its bowl and stem like the leavings of innumerable smokes. But, for the Indian, there was another mystery—the making of a pipe. The cutting and carving of the stone, the hollowing and firing of the stem, the decoration of the pipe—all this had special significance. Like the Great Spirit's Creation, the pipe too was a universe, and, by making their pipes, the Indians might cautiously approach Godliness.

How to Make a Calumet

In the 1800s, when Catlin lived with the Sioux, pipe making was a combination of artistry and old-fashioned drudgery. Catlin wrote in 1841:

The Indians shape out the bowls of their pipes from the solid stone with nothing but a knife. The Indian makes the hole in the bowl of the pipe by drilling into it a hard stick shaped to the desired size, with a quantity of sharp sand and water, kept constantly in the hole, subjecting him therefore to a very great labor and the necessity of much patience.

Nevertheless, the arduous labor was worth the effort, for the well-wrought calumet, as pleasant to look at as it is to smoke, was frequently a tribal heirloom. And now, as Indian pipes become scarcer and scarcer and the old ways are lost, a calumet is a thing of rare and special beauty.

Regrettably, it is most difficult to obtain a piece of true red pipestone today; the merchants who once dealt in Indian supplies are, for all practical purposes, defunct, and the old quarries are now in government possession. Many excellent substitutes, however, can be readily located just about everywhere. Generally speaking, any mineral that can be carved is usable, the best being steatite, or soapstone. True to its name, it has a "soapy" texture and is usually found in and along streams and rivers. A grayish color, it will turn black with use and exposure. Best of all, though, it is very easy to carve, being so soft. Once the stone has been worked, however, it becomes harder and harder and so makes a perfect material for a pipe bowl.

Other possibilities include sand- and limestone and some varieties of marble. One tribe, for instance, cut their pipes from a very hard marble in order to make the walls of the bowl exceedingly thin, yet strong. At night or in a darkened lodge, the glowing *kinnikinnik* would make the bowl luminous and so produce a rather remarkable effect.

To make the bowl, get a piece of suitable stone that measures approximately three inches wide by one inch deep by seven

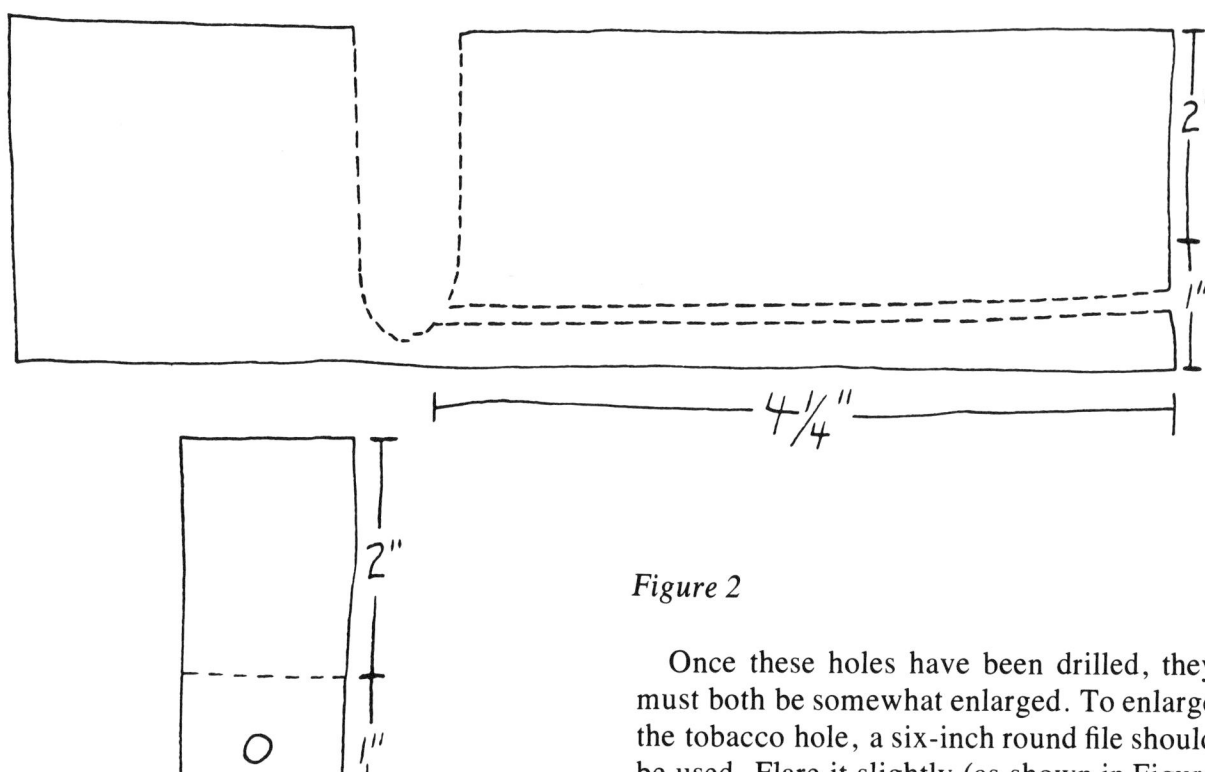

Figure 2

inches long. To trim down larger pieces, you can use a hacksaw. (A coarse blade—eighteen teeth per inch—is best for rough cuts.)

Chuck a half-inch masonry bit into your drill and proceed to bore the tobacco hole as indicated in Figure 1. If you're concerned about exceeding the two-and-five-eighths-inch depth, mark it off on the drill bit with a crayon, measuring the depth up from the point. To ensure an accurate bore, always remember to drill downwards.

Next, reclamp the piece of stone in the vise so that the smoke hole can be drilled. Chuck an eighth-inch masonry bit into your drill and bore to a depth of four and a quarter inches, or until the bit reaches the bowl. (See Figure 2.) Try to drill precisely, as the smoke hole should meet the tobacco hole at a ninety-degree angle.

Once these holes have been drilled, they must both be somewhat enlarged. To enlarge the tobacco hole, a six-inch round file should be used. Flare it slightly (as shown in Figure 3) to allow easy filling and cleaning. The smoke hole, too, must be enlarged to admit the insertion of the stem. This should be done with a quarter-inch masonry bit to a depth of three-quarter inches (as shown in Figure 3).

Next, the bowl must be cut away from the block. To do this, score the block as indicated in Figure 4. Then, with a hacksaw, cut carefully along the lines. The bowl is now rough-finished.

To complete, round off all the edges with a flat file; for the areas around the base of the bowl proper a flexible round file is best. Leave the bottom pretty flat so that the pipe will be able to sit upright without any support.

For a smooth surface, use emery cloth, then steel wool until all the file scratches have been removed. If you'd like a glossy finish, rub some hot beeswax onto the stone

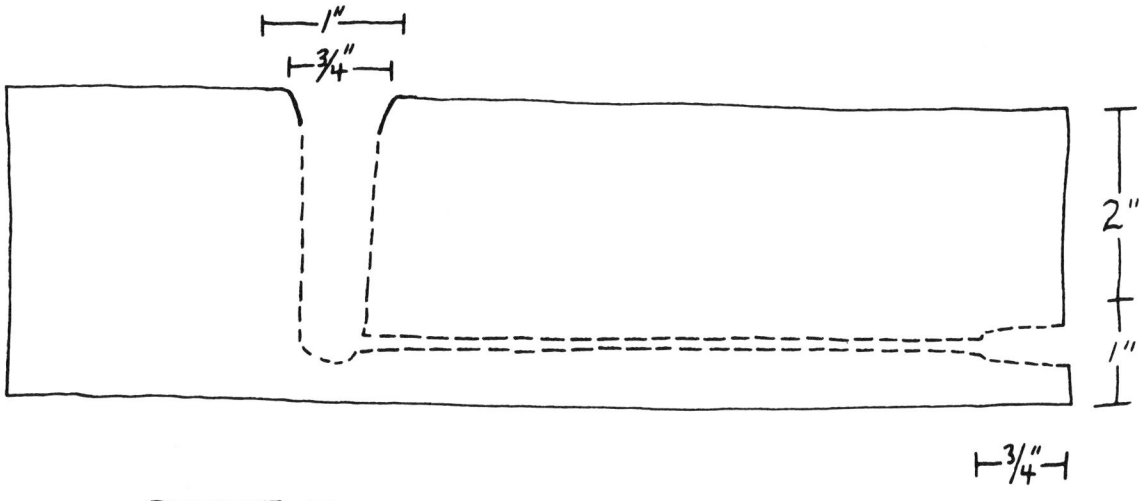

Figure 3

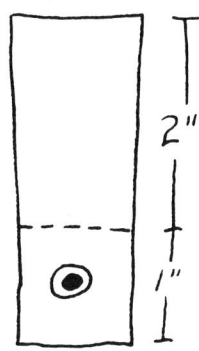

and polish the bowl with a soft cloth. However, if the stone is at all comely now, with use its appearance will mature strikingly.

. . . And the Stem

To make an authentic pipestem, you've got to use the right kind of tree branch. The criterion is this: The branch must have a nice pulpy pith that can easily be bored out to make the smoke hole. There are only a few trees that fill this requirement, though they are pretty much scattered all over.

Undoubtedly the finest of all, the ash was used by Indians whenever and wherever possible. Once its pith has been extracted, a clean eighth-inch smoke hole remains, making a perfect pipe stem. If you can't find an ash, however, don't fret: sumac or witch hazel will serve nearly as well, the only slight drawback being that the smoke hole will be a bit larger. Once one of these trees has been located, cut a two-foot length from as straight a branch as you can find; a one-inch diameter is perfect.

The next matter for consideration is how to put a hole through a two-foot-long branch. For the Indians, there were three methods. The earliest and most primitive was to split the branch lengthwise, carefully dig out the pith with a knife blade, and then glue the two halves back together again. To better secure the stem, it was frequently reinforced with rawhide lashing. A pipe stem made in this fashion, however, tends to warp and thus become drafty. What we need is an airtight stem, and the notion of splitting the branch must be discarded.

To make airtight stems, the Indians had two methods. The more clever one was to capture a wood-boring grub, a small worm-

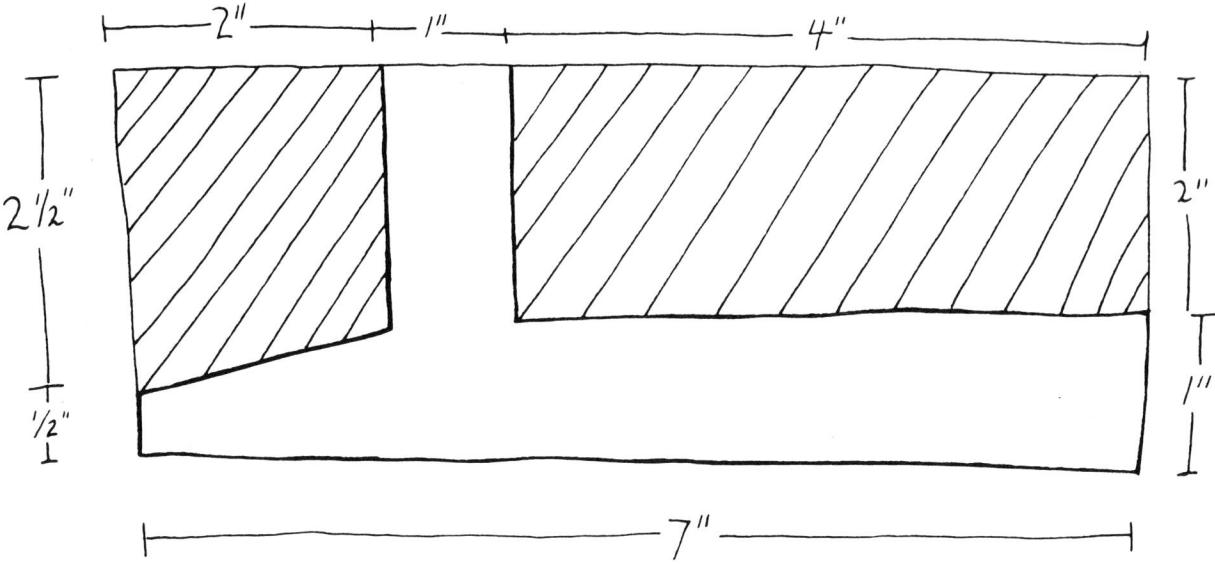

Figure 4

like creature that bores through wood quite rapidly if given the proper impetus. What the Indians used to do was this: They'd dig out about an inch of the pith at one end of the branch and then drop the grub inside. Then they'd seal it inside with a little mud or clay. Once the grub was trapped inside the stem, it was suspended over a hot fire, grub end down; the grub, anxious to flee the heat, would then begin to bore furiously away from the fire. Thus, because the soft pith was the path of least resistance, in a little while the grub would emerge triumphantly at the opposite end of the stick, and the hole would be effortlessly bored. This method however rests on the contingency that a wood-boring grub is available, which is not always the case.

This leaves the third and most commonly used method: burning out the pith with a hot wire. This method not only bores the hole, it hardens the inside of the stem, making it more heat-resistant and airtight. To burn out the pith, put the tip of a one-foot length of eighth-inch copper wire in a roaring fire until it is as hot as possible. Then, working from both ends, burn out the pith until the branch is hollow. You will have to keep reheating the wire in order to complete the job, but it shouldn't take more than half an hour or so. When the smoke hole is bored, whittle the ends as shown in Figure 5 to make the mouthpiece and the extension for insertion into the bowl.

To finish the pipestem in the beautiful traditional way,

remove the bark carefully and rub grease [animal fat] all over the sides of the stick. Now hold it over a fire of green hardwood until the stick turns uniformly dark. While it is still hot, rub it briskly with a rough cloth to produce a smooth, shining pipestem, brown in color ranging from medium to dark approaching black, depending upon how

old Indian carving trick, here slightly updated, must be used. Use a branch two feet long by one inch in diameter, as before, but

note that the pipestem is to be flat for ten inches at the pipe end, and then is to spiral for fourteen inches at the mouth end. After the hole has been burned through the center, remove the bark, tear up some adhesive tape into strips three eighths of an inch in width, and stick these strips on the stem [as shown in Figure 7]. Two strips are placed opposite each other at the pipe end as

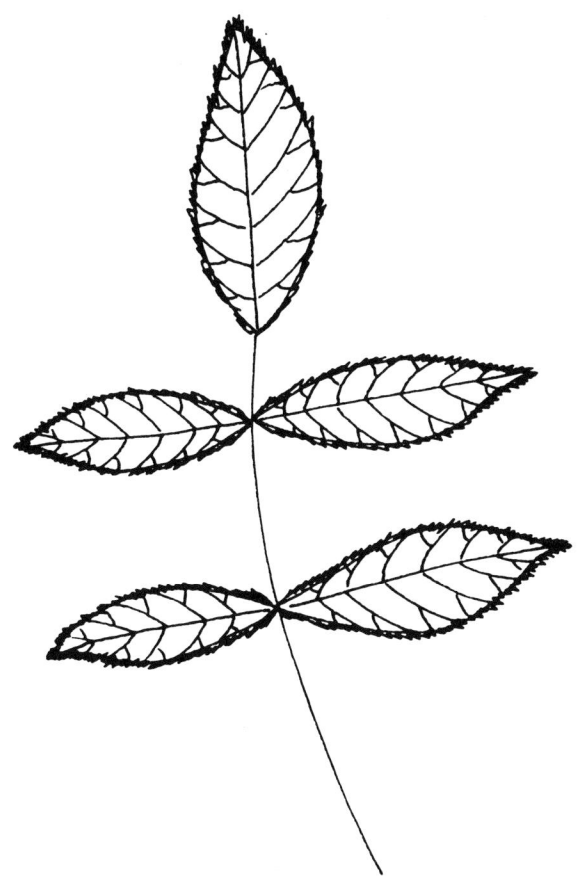

A Twig of Ash; Tree: 40–60 feet tall; Twigs: smooth, ash-colored; Leaves: 3–5 inches long, dark green.

long it was kept in the fire. The darker brown is preferable, but do not leave it over the fire so long that the wood becomes charred, for we seek to produce a stem of shining smoothness. This is the Indian's method of fire coloration.

For some rituals, especially those in which the pipe held supreme significance, special stems were used. These twisted or spiralled stems (see Figure 6), wonders of graceful craftsmanship, are easier to make than it would seem. To make the twisted stem, an

A Twig of Witch-Hazel; Tree: 20–30 feet tall; Twigs: roughish, olive-gray; Leaves: dark green tops, light green bottoms

Figure 5

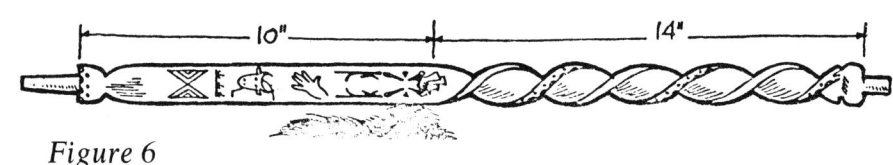

Figure 6

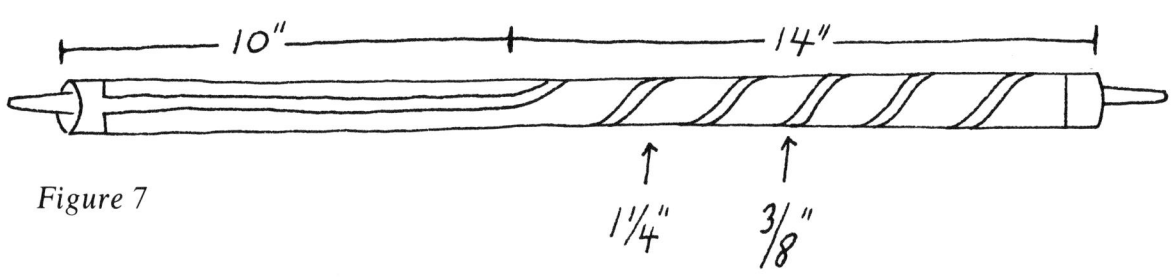

Figure 7

shown, and then are spiralled around it at the mouth end. Note that the spirals are an inch and a quarter apart. The adhesive tape serving as a guide, all we have to do is to hollow out the areas between the tape, and whittle the pipe end down to flat surfaces even with the tape. Excavate the hollows between the spiraled tape to a nice, even, sweeping curve, removing as much wood as possible to make the stem light, trim, and dressy; when the work is all completed, remove the tape.*

*From Bernard S. Mason's *Woodcraft* (A. S. Barnes, Inc.)

HOOKAHS AND HUBBLE-BUBBLES

The Nargeeleh

In 1680, the learned Kircher, in an attempt to mollify the noxious effects of smoking, proposed that

if the gluttons vomiting fire, who relish the horrible and bad-smelling herb, were to pass the smoky nourishment through a phial containing wine or some odoriferous liquid, they would find this fume more palatable, and they could more quickly free their mouths from the pestilential exhalation.

He then proceeded, for he was a scientist, to prove that tobacco smoke is indeed impermeable by water, thus verifying the practicality of a device that could revolutionize the smoking world. Well, the world was not so small then as it is now: How was he to know that water pipes were the customary mode of smoking in Persia, India, and parts of Africa?

Generally, the Persians are attributed with the invention of this splendiferous device, though very early accounts of Africa relate how some of the natives would fill their mouths with water before smoking, making themselves into human water pipes. The Persians, however, were the first to manufacture the actual instrument. The Arabs of Hindustan, in turn, picked it up from their Persian neighbors and so, by trade and travel, the water pipe circulated to Africa where it was gratefully used to smoke the harsh and intoxicating *bhang*.

The most rudimentary sort of water pipe, called the *nargeeleh* after the Arabic for "coconut," supposedly owes its origin to a Persian fellow by the name of Thatmass. The story, related by a traveler in the 1850s, runs that poor Thatmass "was troubled with a complaint which rendered him a nuisance to himself and to others in whose company he happened to be. After a great many failures, he invented the *nargeeleh*, in whose soft slumberous gurgle his own infirmity was drowned." Indeed, the *nargeeleh* does emit a singular sound, something like its pejorative name: hubble-bubble.

Fashioned from a coconut or, less frequently, a glass flagon, gourd, or cucumber, *nargeelehs* were decidedly modish in Persian coffee houses around the turn of the seventeenth century.

Said John Fryer in the 1670s:

They are modelled after the nature of our theatres, that every one may sit around, and suck choice tobacco out of long Malabar canes, fastened to crystal bottles . . . after this sort they are mightily pleased: for putting fragrant and delightful flowers into the water, upon every attempt to draw tobacco, the water bubbles, and makes them dance in various figures, which both qualifies the heat of the smoke, and creates together a pretty sight.

Accommodating a sophisticated clientele, coffee houses used crystal bottles rather than the ordinary and customary coconut.

Perhaps the least liberated of all females, the Persian women used to cater to their men's predilection for the water. It seems that the Persian men liked to drink the water after the tobacco or *hasheesh* smoke had filtered through it, leaving behind an oily residue that flavored the water to their liking. The women, consequently, were frequently made to smoke five or six pipefuls in rapid succession, while the men waited idly by for their drink.

Melodious and a milestone in women's lib, the *nargeeleh* makes a unique addition to anyone's collection.

How to Make a Nargeeleh

To make a *nargeeleh* after the traditional mode, select either a comely coconut or a shapely gourd. If you prefer coconuts (the more durable, hence practical), select one that is as symmetrically perfect as possible, nicely rounded at the top and neatly tapered toward its bottom. If, on the other hand, you happen to be a gourd fancier, be certain to select one of the so-called "tear-drop" variety rather than one of those squat fellows. Whatever your choice, however, try to obtain the biggest of the bunch, for these are usually the toughest and, therefore, most appropriate to our purpose.

Once a suitable specimen has been selected, it must be properly seasoned. Ripe, the fruit is of no value: it must be thoroughly dried before we proceed. When drying your fruit, do so in the shade since the sun will hasten its deterioration drastically. A dark and moderately cool place is best. O yes, if you're using a coconut, be sure to pierce its top to allow the milk to run off before attempting to dry it. After several weeks of drying (though ten days is sometimes sufficient), tap your gourd or nut with your knuckle. If the sound you hear is hollow and resonant, then it's safe to say that you may proceed with the making.

For our bowl, we will use the tube pipe, or *chillum*, because it is the traditional way and because it is the best. Complete instructions for the manufacture of same can be found in Chapter II of this book. The wooden *chillum*, because it is light and our other materials are relatively delicate, is recommended strongly. By itself, however, the chillum is insufficient, for it must be long enough to extend into the water. Hence, an extension is required.

To make an extension for your *chillum*, go to your nearest craft and hobby shop and pick up about one foot of quarter-inch brass tubing. If your craft shop doesn't carry it, they will be able to order it; otherwise, you can try the hardware store. To fit the tubing inside the *chillum*, slightly crimp one end of it and, with a twisting motion, slide the tubing up inside the chillum. In most instances, the tubing need only extend about a half inch into the *chillum*. The fit here, because both the hole and the tubing have the same quarter-inch diameters, ought to be very snug. If, however, the fit is too loose, wind a bit of electrical tape around the end of the tubing; this will most assuredly take up the slack.

The length of the tubing is determined by the size of your coconut: It must extend into the water yet not touch the bottom. (See Figure 1.) In that illustration, for example, the length of the tubing is three and a half inches. (One-half inch extends into the *chillum* and three inches extend into the water.) Thus, the tubing sits one-half inch from the bottom of the coconut, a perfect distance. Once these specifications have been derived according to the dimensions of your own nut, it is next to fit this unit securely into it. To do so, bore a hole approximately three-quarters of an inch in diameter into the top of the coconut. This way, the *chillum's* "bowl" should sit atop the nut nicely, its "stem" out of sight inside.

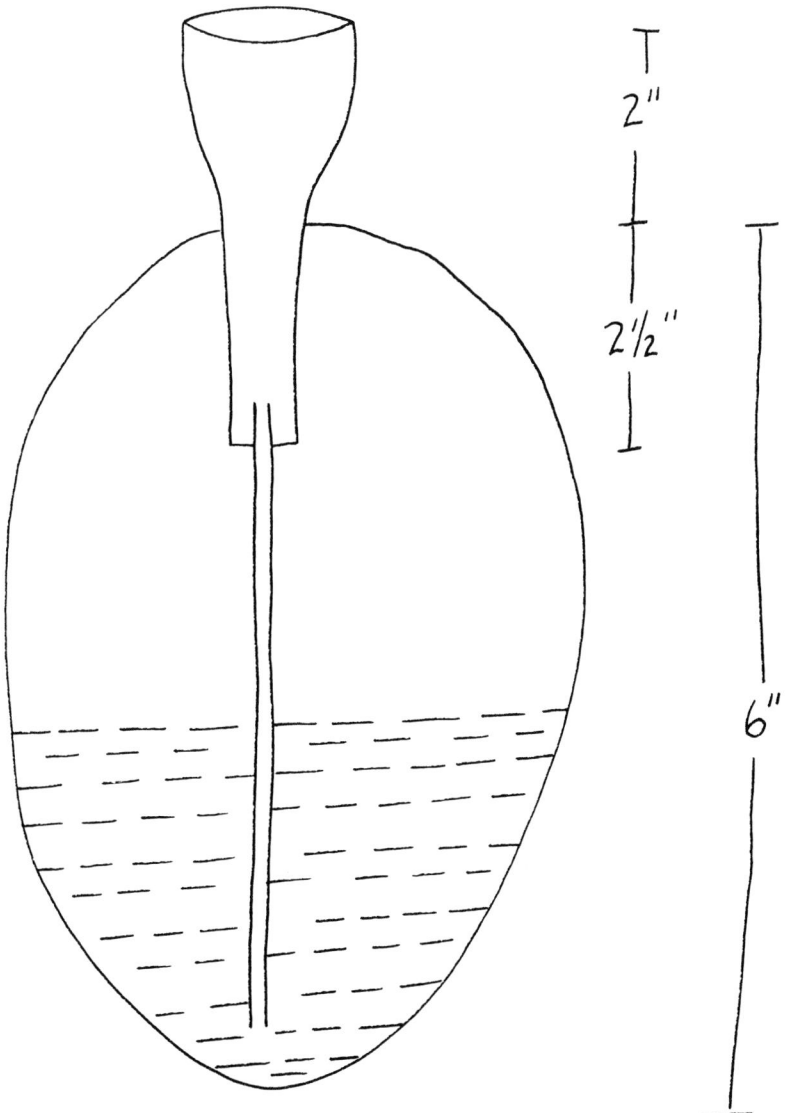

Figure 1

To ensure a tight fit at this junction, for it ought to be as airtight as possible, twist some ordinary string around the *chillum* at the point where it meets the coconut and tie it off firmly. After filling the nut with water (about half full), wet the string, too. Then, push the *chillum* into the nut, and you will find that the wetted string makes a fine seal; unlike a glue, it makes for an easy removal of the bowl.

Once the bowl has been fitted, remove it temporarily and take out your drill again. This time we are going to drill diagonally into the side of the nut so that the stem might be inserted. (See Figure 2.) Although there are numerous materials that might be employed for the stem (from rubber to plastic to brass), I strongly urge the use of bamboo. Naturally hollow and available in nearly any size, it makes a superior stem (in contrast to

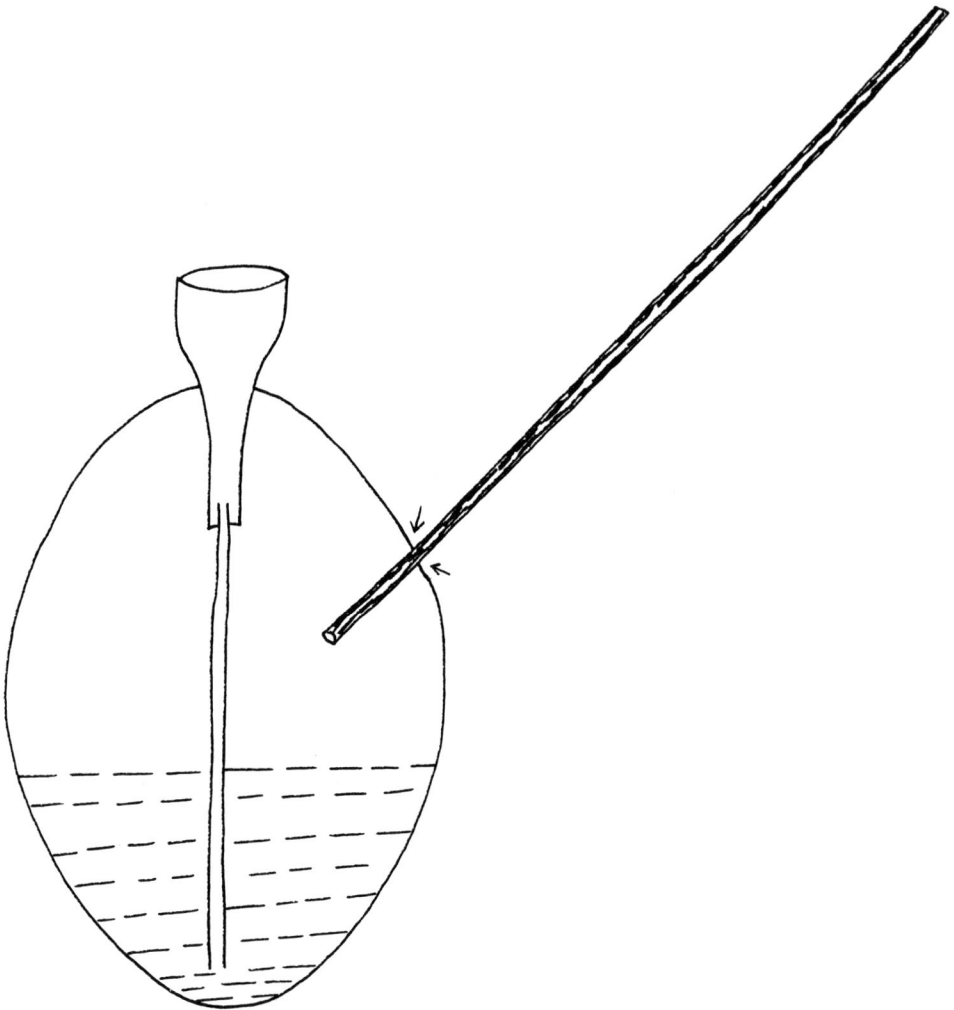

Figure 2

plastic or brass, at least). Once again, be certain to make it a tight fit. Here, because it is not necessary to remove the stem (pipe cleaners are sold in enormous sizes these days), it is advisable to glue the stem in place. To do this, slide the stem into the coconut about an inch or so and apply a good waterproof glue to the outside perimeter as indicated by the two arrows in Figure 2. This not only ensures airtightness but adds a certain steadfastness to the pipe that is often lacking otherwise. Put the bowl back in place after filling the pipe with water, and the *nargeeleh* is ready for firing up.

An amusing variation of this portable *nargeeleh* is the standing or upright *nargeeleh*. This, the type in which the Turkish grandees took so much delight at their coffee houses and private residences, offers the added attraction of luxury: The smoker need not hold the coconut in his hands, and what's more, he may partake of his favorite poison while reclining on his favorite bed of cushions.

To make this nobleman's *nargeeleh*, we have but to make a stand in which it can sit

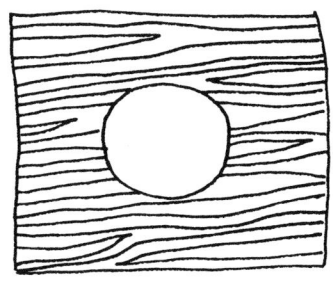

Figure 3

clear pine that measures three inches square and, in the center of it, bore a one-inch diameter hole with a wood-boring bit. (See Figure 3.) This diameter, of course, may vary according to the size of your nut, though an inch generally accommodates all and to extend the length of the stem to one compatible with the smoker's pleasure. To make the *nargeeleh* stand, take a piece of

Figure 4

comers. To this square with the hole in the center, we must afix four legs, one at each corner. Two-inch lengths of one inch by one inch stock nailed to the corners are fine. Sand, stain, or paint the stand according to your preference. To complete this elegant device, extend the stem to a length of anywhere from three to nine feet; once securely attached, you may indulge in true luxury with a minimum of fuss. (See Figure 4.)

The other alternative, the *nargeeleh* constructed from a gourd, is speedily manufactured. In the gourd's bulbous end, drill a three-quarter-inch hole and secure the *chillum* unit as previously described. To effect a

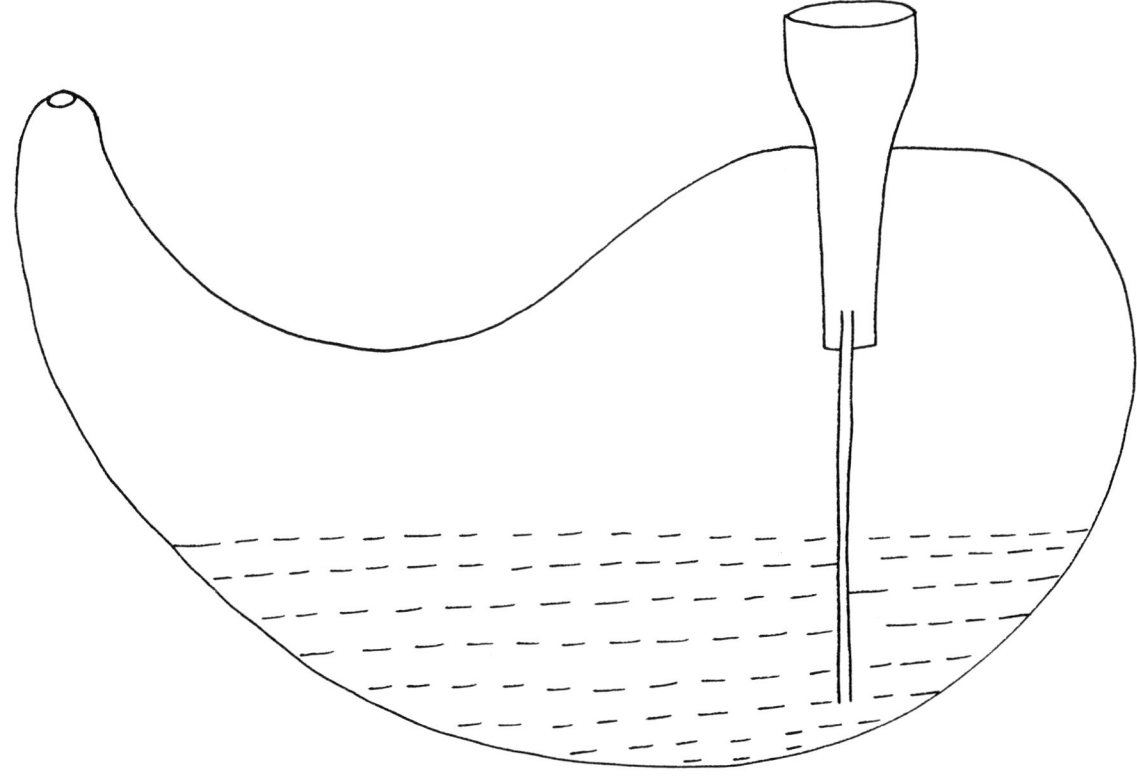

Figure 5

stem, simply bore a small opening in the gourd's narrow end (see Figure 5), and the pipe is ready to go. If you like, a length of bamboo may be inserted and glued into this hole, though the gourd's unique shape makes it a natural pipe without any workshop persuasion.

Chinese Water Pipes

A nation of expert metal smiths, the Chinese have improvised elegant water pipes out of brass, silver, and gold. Operating on the same principle as the *nargeeleh*, these pipes are much more intricate in their design—some made into herons or elephants (pictured) or simply graceful designs. Others offer meticulous scroll-work designs of birds, flowers, and landscapes—all to enrich an already luxuriant pipe.

Situated behind the stem, in six of these specimens, is a separate chamber for tobacco; as seen in one, the interior of the lid is ornately inscribed. A cleansing brush and ember tongs are also provided, making the pipe a paragon of efficiency as well as artistry.

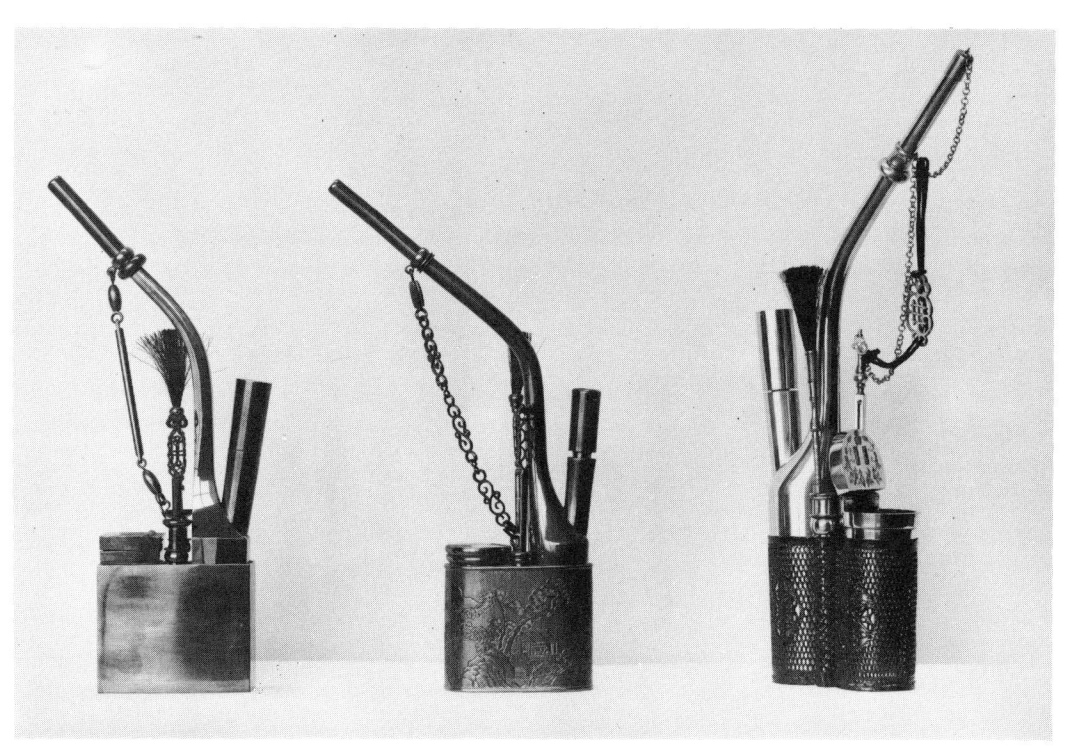

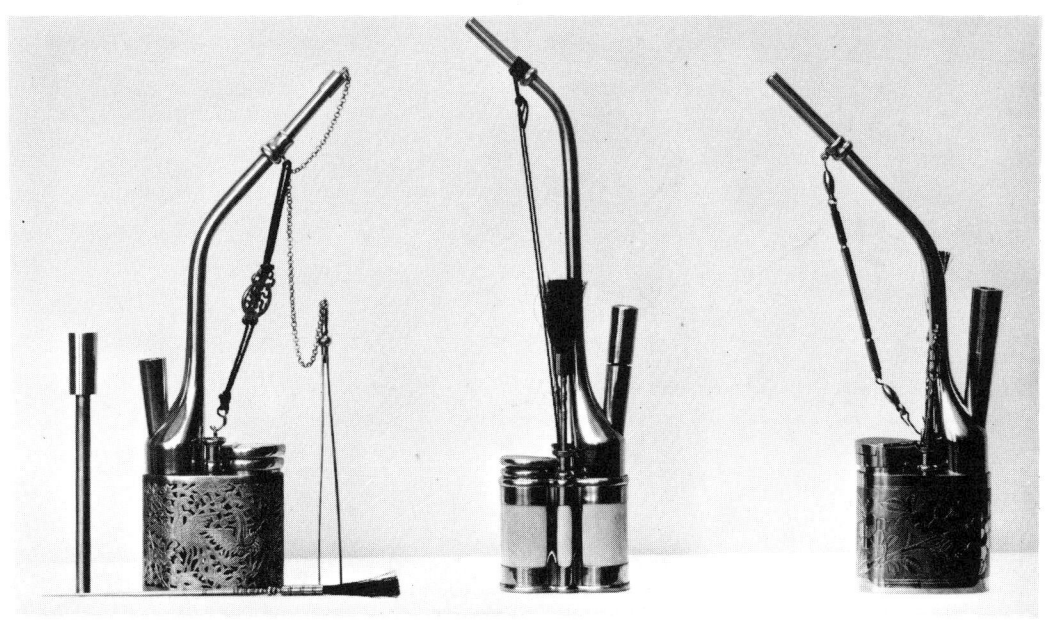

*Chinese Water-Pipes: a Happy Blend of Beauty and Practicality
(Courtesy of the Field Museum of Natural History, Chicago)*

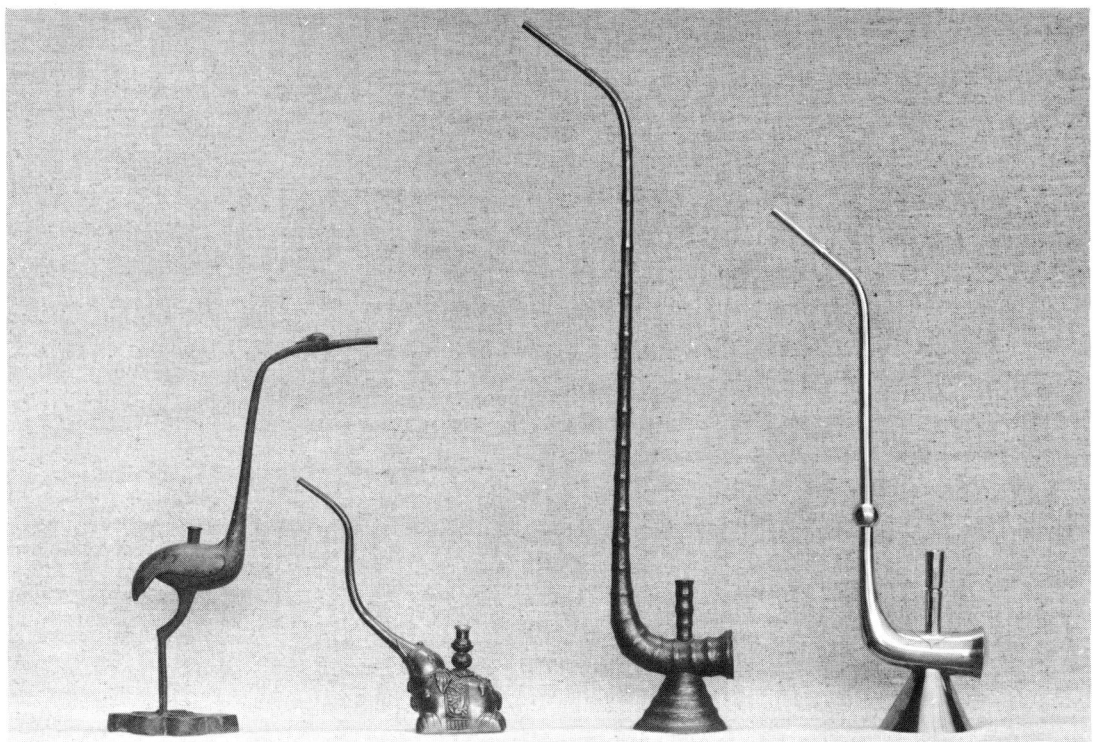

Fanciful Water Pipes of the Far East (Courtesy of the Field Museum of Natural History, Chicago)

The Hookah

Last of the long pipes, properly so called, comes the hookah or water pipe. But if this is to be smoked well it must be with its appropriate tobacco, prepared in the orthodox manner, and lighted and kept burning by charcoal. Wherefore he who smokes a hookah should have a slave whose sole duty is the care thereof, else it is a weariness, and productive rather of pain than pleasure. But if the slave understands his office well, then it shall give thee joy, both by reason of the twistings and writhings of the tube and the sight of the smoke curling forth at so great a distance. Wherefore, when I shall become possessed of gold and silver in abundance, I will build me a house with a great hall about the size of a tennis court. And at one end there shall be a dais, with cushions of precious stuff in the Eastern Manner, whereon I will sit me down. But at the other, nigh unto the roof, shall be a gallery with mighty hookahs thereon, the least of which shall hold a full pound of tobacco. And from them, in many twisting convolutions, shall their tubes go forth, yea, even unto the cushioned dais shall they go; and seated there with my friends I shall truly smoke and partake of the real and divine energy.

—Arthur Machen
The Anatomy of Tobacco

The Hamlet of pipes, the hookah is the celebrated author of "pipe dreams," a capricious prince in whose "twistings and writhings" ordinary reality dissipates like smoke itself.

Once the gem of Persia alone, the hookah was swiftly adopted by all who encountered its enticing charms, not the least of whom were the British who occupied India. They, in fact, did have servants, called *hookah-burdars*, whose sole duty was to attend to their masters' hookahs. These gentlemen not only kept the pipe in perfect repair but freshened the water as so required or requested, prepared the smoking mixture according to his master's taste, lit the tobacco and kept it burning evenly, and even transported it to social functions at which he would carry out his charge (though occasionally *hookah-burdars* were provided by the host). Such servants were regarded with respect, and those especially adept in their station were prized much as one might today prize a fine French chef.

Indeed, it required more than a modicum of skill to properly attend to a hookah. The tobacco, first of all, had to be reduced to a powder that was then kneaded into a flat cake with molasses and water. This was placed in the bowl beneath a circular disc of baked clay called a *tawa*. Atop this was set a glowing coal much like that used now to ignite cone incense. Then, as the clay disc heated, the mixture would burn evenly and at a leisurely pace. Furthermore, the water or wine employed had to be scrupulously selected in order to enhance the robustness or subtleties of the smoke. Spices, flavorings, and flowers were put to use as the master's appetite dictated. In all, a rather tedious balance hung between a good smoke and a memorable one.

Characteristic of all hookahs are long snake-like stems properly called narbeeshes. These range in length from two to thirty feet, the ideal length being that which suits the personal bent of one's mind. Some, for instance, would choose to smoke in a reclined attitude, carelessly drifting in a sea of soft cushions; for such smokers the twenty- to thirty-foot *narbeesh* is appropriate. Other, more deliberative types, might enjoy pondering while sucking on a short *narbeesh,* say three to five feet. Ultimately of course such matters must be resolved according to personal propensities.

How to make a hookah

To make a hookah, it is first necessary to acquire a portly vessel whose fanciful countenance will add immeasurably to your smoking pleasure. Ornate vases with wide necks, old-time New England bean crocks, hammered brass spittoons, and cut crystal liqueur decanters are among the limitless possibilities. When making a hookah, never settle for the mediocre when you can obtain better: The time and effort that you will spend truly justifies a magnificent vessel. Too, this will be your most costly item, the remainder of the materials being purchased quite inexpensively or else foraged from basements, attics, etc. When selecting said vessel, there is something else you ought to consider: that is, shall it be an opaque or a transparent one. There is something to be said for both. With the opaque vessel you generally find it to be more decorative; it is often painted, gilded, or otherwise adorned. The transparent, on the other hand, is usually much plainer in appearance—at first. When, however, you sprinkle flowers on the surface of the water therein and watch them dance as the smoke bubbles through and then curls upward in fascinating patterns, you might think otherwise. To this problem there is but one solution: Build yourself a pair.

Your next acquisition must be a proper stopper; that is, a cork that will fit snugly into the vessel's mouth. Stoppers of both cork and rubber are acceptable, the former readily purchased at most hardware stores in varying sizes and shapes, the latter secured from laboratory-supply merchants. You should also know that cork comes in different quality grades, and it is always best to obtain the finest grade available. Good cork is very tight, close-grained, and rather hard. If you cannot locate a size that will perfectly fit your vessel, purchase a size too large: Cork can easily and accurately be cut down to size with a coping saw. If, on the other hand, rubber is your preference, again be certain to get a good quality as these, too, come in varying grades. Above all, no matter what material you use, be sure that the stopper sits snugly in the mouth so that you have an airtight fit.

The next material needed is a short section of fancy wooden dowel. Available at lumber yards and building-supply houses, these fancy dowels are commonly used for furniture legs, wall hangings, towel racks, etc. Pick a pattern you like, but in choosing its dimensions a good rule to follow is this: The dowel's overall diameter ought to be about one-third that of the stopper's, and its height should be about equal to the stopper's diameter. For example, if your stopper is three inches in diameter (as is the one used for illustration), then the dowel's diameter ought to be about an inch, while its height should be about three inches. Serving as the hookah's neck, the dowel makes a handsome and sturdy support for the bowl. It can be either stained or painted according to your own design.

In Chapter II, directions for making the tube pipe, or *chillum*, are given. A slightly modified version of the wooden tube pipe will serve as the hookah's bowl. To make this bowl, follow the procedure as outlined in that chapter, altering the specifications as indicated by Figure 1. An inch wide at the top, it tapers to a uniform thickness of one-half inch. Extending for a distance of one

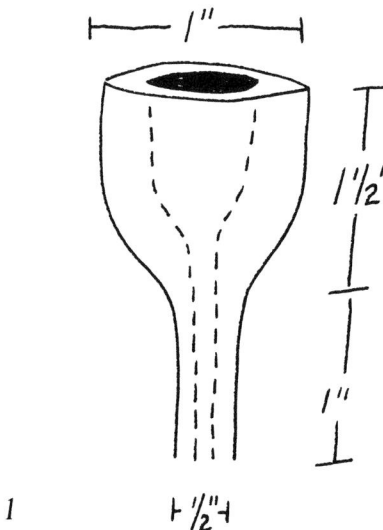

Figure 1

inch, the stem part of the *chillum* must be as even as possible, for it will be fitted into the neck. This is a fairly precise operation, and you should proceed cautiously, using finer and finer sandpaper until the diameter of one-half inch is achieved uniformly throughout. Never paint, varnish, or shellac any part of the *chillum* as the bowl must be allowed to breath or it will invariably crack. If you like, it might be stained or just lightly oiled with boiled linseed oil. At this point, you should have four items: a vessel, a stopper, a neck, and a bowl.

Our next task is to fashion the circular metal disc that will fit just beneath the bowl. Used both as a stray spark catcher as well as a tray on which to rest matches, coals, tongs, smoking mixture, etc., it also enchances the pipe's exotic appearance. On a three-inch square of thin tin or copper, scribe a circle as indicated in Figure 2. For best results use a compass. Then, chuck a half-inch twist drill (or, if you haven't one, a half-inch masonry bit) into your drill and bore a hole directly in the center of the circle. After this has been done, use tin snips to cut out the circles and a mill file to trim any sharp edges that may

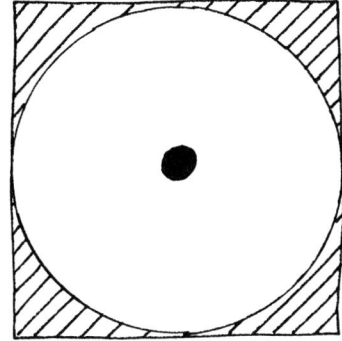

Figure 2

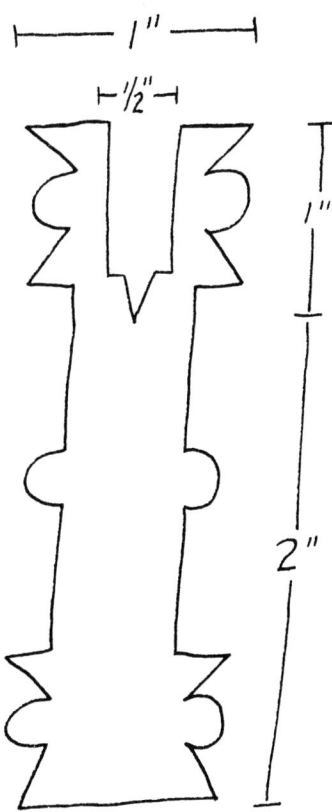

Figure 3

have resulted from the cutting. This piece may either be painted with enamel paints or left as is. Then, slide it onto the stem of the *chillum*, and it should stop at the point where the actual bowl begins to take shape.

Next, clamp the dowel securely in your vise so that it is vertical to the floor and, using a half-inch wood-boring bit, drill as indicated in figure 3. A depth of one inch should be just about perfect to accomodate the chillum's stem, although it's better to drill a bit deeper than be caught shallow. We also need a smoke hole through the dowel and, since the dowel is already clamped, now is a good time to drill it. Using a quater inch twist drill, bore through to the other end of the dowel. It should now be hollow and look pretty much like figure 4.

We are now ready to set the bowl into the neck. Because the diameter of each is the same (one half inch), it should be an exceedingly tight fit which, of course, is good and desirable. If, however, for any reason, the neck and bowl do not come together properly, this situation can be quickly remedied. If the hole in the neck is too large, wrap a strip of electrical tape around the stem of the bowl and this will take up the slack. Two, or even three layers of tape can be used to build up the stem still further if necessary. On the other hand, if the stem of the *chillum* is too large and, consequently, penetration is impossible, first try rubbing a bit of bar soap on the stem of the *chillum*. Sometimes this dry lubricant will provide just enough lubrication to effect the union. If this doesn't work, the stem will have to be carefully sandpapered down. Again, work cautiously, making cer-

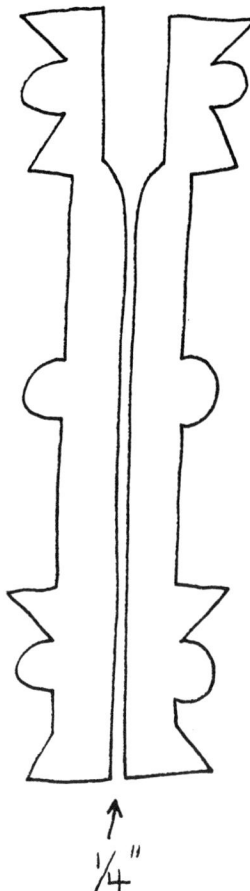

Figure 4

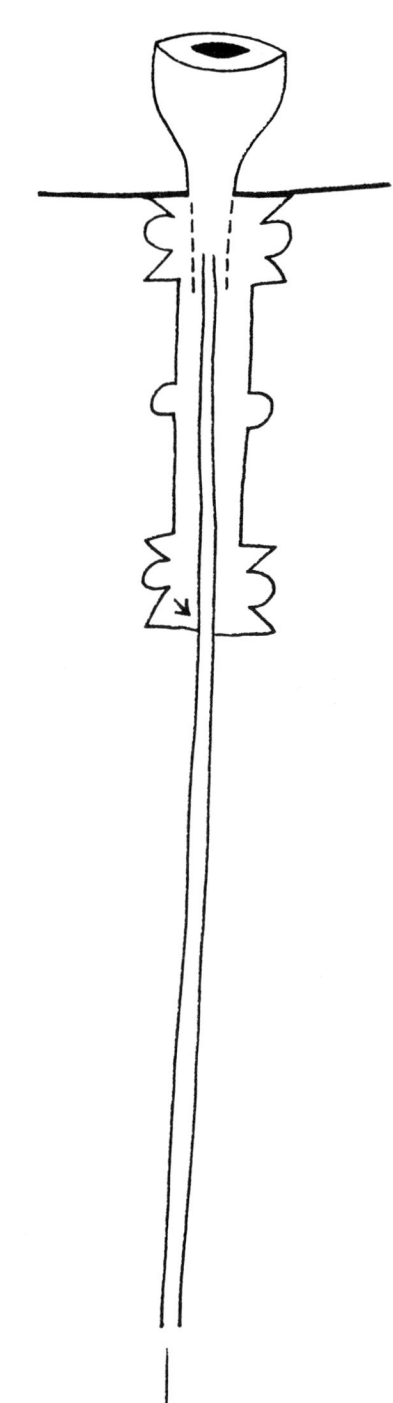

Figure 5

tain not to take off too much: our goal is a perfectly air- and watertight fit.

Once the neck has been secured to the bowl (and the metal disc securely sandwiched in between), we must next insert a length of quarter-inch brass tubing up through the other end of the dowel so that it enters into the smoke channel of the *chillum*. (See Figure 5). We need this extension so that the smoke will be drawn not merely into the vessel but all the way down below the surface of the water. To slide the tubing up into the neck unit, slightly crimp one end of it and twist it upward until it is about a half inch into the *chillum* itself. Once this end is securely in place (a piece of electrical tape might be needed to ensure absolute tightness—see arrow in illustration), cut off the other end so that the tubing will reach within an inch of the bottom of the vessel. To determine the overall length of the tubing, measure the combined height of the neck (without the bowl) and the vessel, then subtract an inch and a half. For example, if the height of your vessel is sixteen inches and the height of the neck three inches, then the total length of the brass tubing should be seventeen and a half inches. Once this step has been completed, the neck assembly is finished.

Before we can proceed with the next step, inserting the neck assembly into the stopper, you must determine the number of *narbeeshes* or stems that you want. Any number from one to six is possible. In Figure 6, three *narbeesh* holes and one neck assembly hole have been drilled. They are all a quarter inch in diameter and should be drilled with a quarter-inch twist drill while the cork or stopper is clamped in your vise. Drill the holes so that the one for the neck

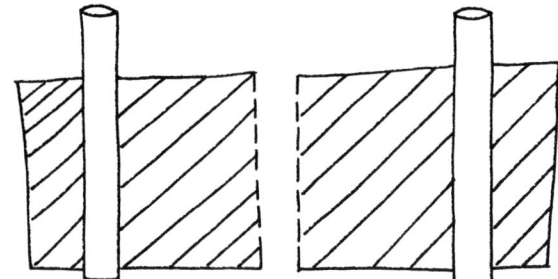

Figure 7

assembly is in the exact center of the stopper, and the others symmetrically arranged around it. Once these holes have been bored, slide the neck assembly into the center hole.

In order for the *narbeeshes* to adequately attach to the stopper, we must provide nipples onto which they can be fastened. To do this, slide a small section of quarter-inch brass tubing into each *narbeesh* hole so that about one-half inch protrudes upward and about a sixteenth of an inch extends downward. (See Figure 7). To secure these tubing sections, lightly dab each with a spot of glue before sliding them into their respective holes.

We are now ready to fit the entire assembly into the mouth of the vessel. Carefully lower it into the mouth until the stopper tightens and halts. When this has been effected your hookah should look something similar to Figure 8, and we may now proceed with the making of the *narbeeshes*.

To make a *narbeesh* requires both patience and persistence, but once completed, it will enhance your ego almost as much as your pipe. Of course, one could simply use rubber hose, but I feel that would be out of character; instead, let us strive for the old traditional pipe in its full glory. First, take about a three-foot length of one-quarter-inch

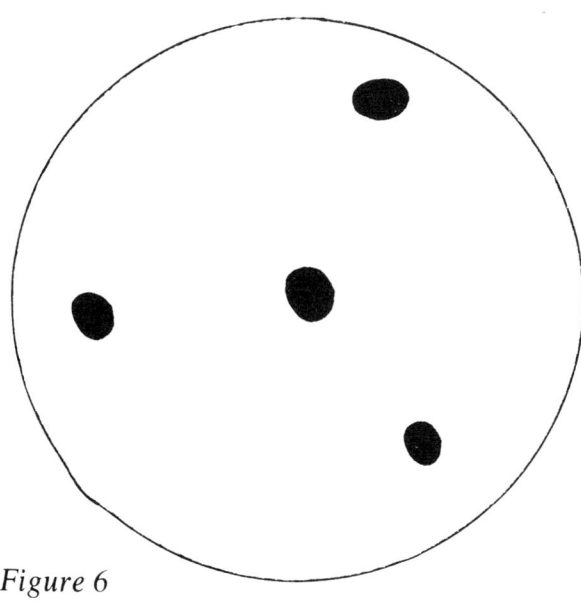

Figure 6

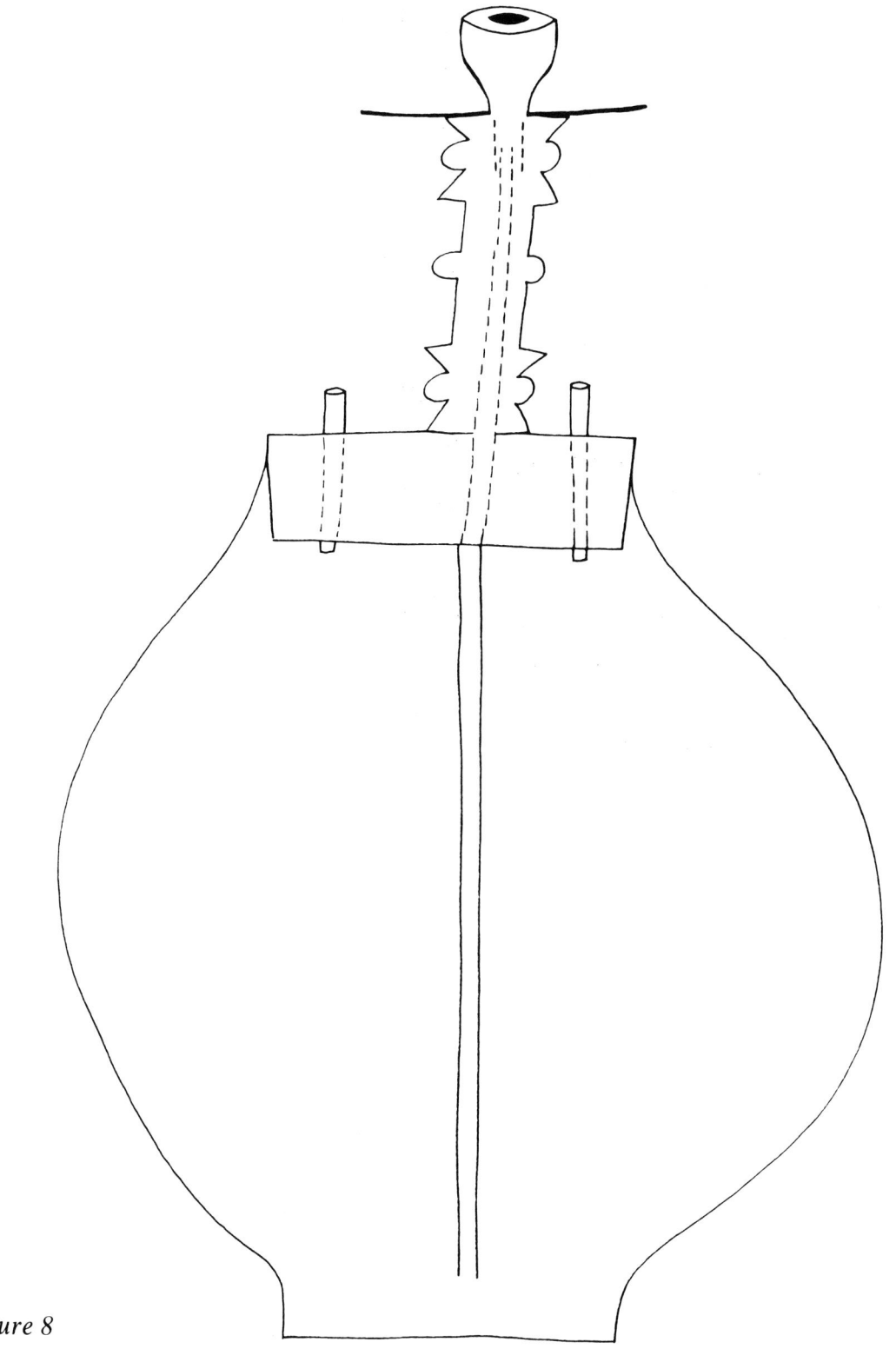

Figure 8

dowel (plain dowel this time) and clamp it lengthwise in your vise so that most of it extends to one side of the vise. (i.e., clamp the dowel so that about two feet eight inches extends to one side.) Around this dowel we are going to wind three layers: fine wire, leather strips, and heavier wire. (See Figure 9.)

We start with the fine wire. To begin, start about an inch from the end and work backward for a few turns; then, reverse direction and wind your way to the vise. This way there will be no loose ends; the procedure should be followed each time a new layer is begun. Be certain to wind each turn as close to the next as possible, so that once you have reached the opposite end the entire dowel is covered with wire and little or no wood is visible in between the turns.

The next layer is leather strips—soft leather cut into strips about a half inch wide. Leather shops are always throwing out scraps or selling them cheaply, and these make perfect material for your strips. Before winding the strips onto the dowel, run each one through a bowl in which you have squeezed a quantity of high-quality water proof glue. Once each strip has passed through the glue, it must be cleaned of all excess by placing the strip between two fingers on your right hand and then pulling it through with your left. The leather strips should be sticky damp, not dripping. To apply, wind tightly as before, being certain that there are no spaces between turns. If necessary, for the leather ensures airtightness, the strips can be overlapped slightly.

Finally, and before the glue has dried, repeat this procedure using a heavier-grade wire than before. This wire, it should be noted, need not be run through glue but should be wound in its naturally dry state. Thus, there will be three layers wound around the dowel. Now, withdraw the dowel, and the first section of the *narbeesh* remains. Once the glue has set, the tube will be flexible yet airtight. To make a longer *narbeesh,* continue this process as many times as needed, three times for a nine footer, five times for a fifteen footer.

To connect the *narbeesh* to the nipple, first wind one or two turns of electrical tape around the nipple to provide a tight grip. Then simply slide the narbeesh onto it. For the other end of the stem, however, we will want to make an appropriate mouthpiece as

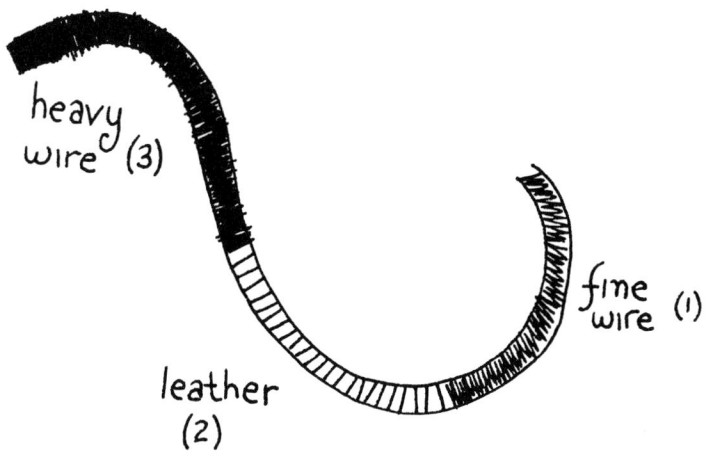

Figure 9

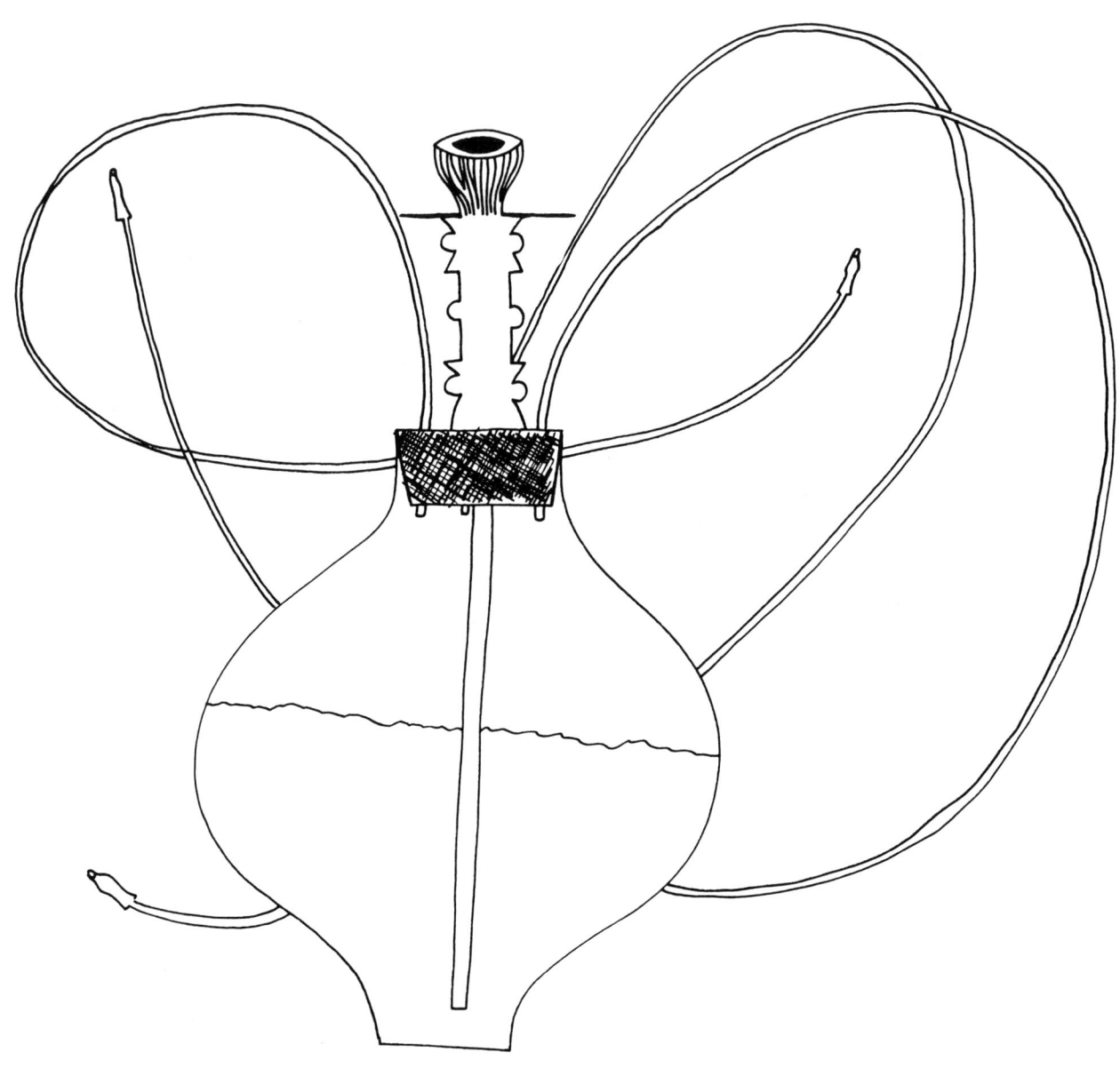

Figure 10

the touch of metal to the lips is incompatible with the succulent smoke that the *narbeesh* will convey to them. Therefore, to make a suitable mouthpiece, take a short (one-inch) piece of half-inch plain dowel and drill a hole through it (lengthwise) one-eighth inch in diameter. Contour, then, as indicated in Figure 10A, using a wood carving knife and sandpaper to finish. Once completed, this mouth piece can be stained, varnished, or painted. To afix the mouthpiece to the stem, simply slide the straight end of it into the *narbeesh* with a touch of glue. A few turns of elctrical tape around this straight part of the mouthpiece will further ensure that it will stay in place.

Another method for making a mouthpiece is to purchase nine-sixteenths-inch wooden beads from your craft and hobby shop. These beads come in different colors, sizes, and shapes. There will be a small hole already in the bead, but this must be enlarged so that it can accommodate the *narbeesh*. Perhaps the best way to do this is to cut a short section of quarter-inch brass tubing. Then slide one end of it up into the bead and leave the other end protruding so that it can, in turn, be pushed into the *narbeesh*. (See Figure 10B.) Again, a dab of glue and/or a few turns of electrical tape might be a good idea.

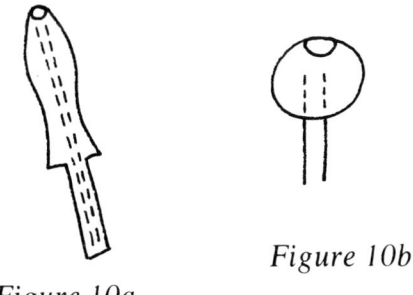

Figure 10a *Figure 10b*

Another handy item to make (several, if you like), as long as you have your wood-carving knife out, is a little slip of wood that can be inserted into the nipple of an unused *narbeesh*. If, perchance, you wish to smoke alone and find that you have two *narbeeshes* too many, simply disconnect the two and slip the little slips of wood into the nipples. These wooden plugs, like corks, will keep the system airtight and enable you to enjoy a solitary smoke.

Napoleon's First Pipe

Constant relates the following anecdote of the great Napoleon, who once took a fancy to smoke, for the purpose of trying a very fine Oriental pipe which had been presented to him by a Turkish or Persian ambassador.

Fire having been brought, it only remained to communicate it to the tobacco, but that could never be effected by the method which his Majesty adopted. He contented himself with alternately opening and shutting his mouth, without attempting to draw in his breath. Oh, the devil! cried he at last, there will be no end of this business. I observed to him that he did it half-heartedly, and showed him how he ought to begin. But the Emperor always returned to his yawning. Wearied by his vain efforts, he at last desired me to light the pipe. I obeyed, and gave it to him. But scarcely had he drawn in a mouthful than the smoke, which he knew not how to expel, turned back into his palate, penetrated into his throat, and came out by his nose and blinded him.

As soon as he recovered his breath, he ejaculated, Take that away from me! What abomination! Oh! the swine!—my stomach turns. *In fact, he felt himself so incommoded for at least an hour, that he renounced forever the pleasure of a habit which he said was only fit to amuse sluggards.*

—From John Baine's
Tobacco in Song and Story

SIX SMOKING PIPES

Clay

In colonial days, when the cultivation of tobacco for export was still in its infancy, a pronounced insufficiency of the weed caused widespread consternation in the mother country. Englishmen, as can be readily gleaned from Chapter I, had taken an undisguised shine to it and clamored for it more and more with each passing day. Unfortunately, because the supply was so severely limited, what tobacco could be had was excessively dear; furthermore, because the monied aristocracy was willing to part with sizable sums to fill their pouches with the precious plant, a veritable dearth of tobacco plagued the general populace. The English, however, are an ingenious race, and they were quick to manifest their characteristic cleverness in this matter. Because they were unable to fatten their tobacco coffers until the American plantations reached large-scale productivity, they decided to decrease the capacity of their pipes and, in short, made their pipe bowls so intolerably tiny as to hold but a score of hefty whiffs. In this agreeable fashion, however, they could go about the pleasurable business of unboxing, ramming, sniffing, and whiffing with greater frequency than if they had employed more capacious pipes. It is for this reason that, when first you meet an English clay, the bowl seems so inordinately small.

In 1598, a gentleman visiting the Southwark Bear Garden observed:

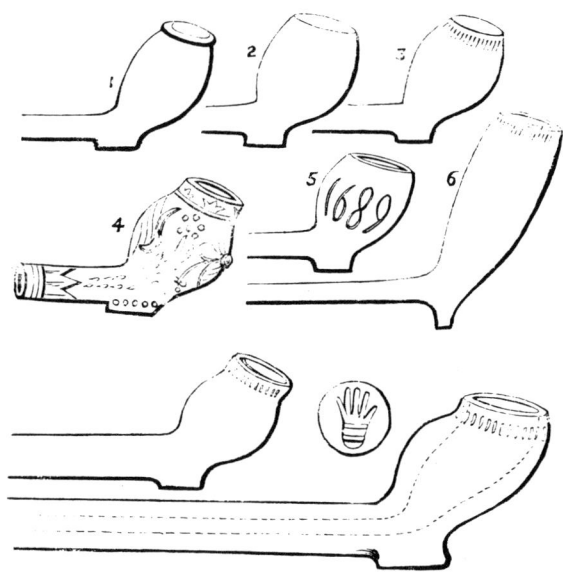

Clay Pipes: Variations on a Theme

"At these spectacles and everywhere else the English are smoking tobacco and in this manner: They have pipes on purpose made of clay, into the further end of which they put the herb, so dry that it may be rubbed into powder, and putting fire to it they draw the smoke into their mouths, which they puff out again through their nostrils, like funnels, along with it plenty of phlegm and defluxion from the head."

Of the clay pipes that were then popular, there were two outstanding types: the cutty and the churchwarden. Of the two, the cutty—or "nose warmer" as it was sometimes called—was by far the shorter, its overall length not exceeding three inches. Generally speaking, the cutty was the common man's pipe, though students at Oxford and Cambridge sometimes affected them due, in part, to their extremely reasonable cost: In 1598 two cutty clays could be had for a penny. In direct contrast to the cutty, the churchwarden was reknowned for its prosperous demeanor. Measuring up to a full twelve inches in length, the churchwarden

An Ornate Case for a Clay Pipe

was frequently the object of excessive decoration. Gold or silver braid, fancifully twisted about its bowl and stem, added that extra touch the cutty lacked. And hardwood and leather cases, too, into which the churchwarden might retire after a day's smoking, added a certain civility that the cutty could never match. In typical fashion, however, the commoners soon began to purchase inexpensive churchwardens in an attempt to ape the aristocrats. Unable to also purchase the expensive cases, however, they pierced small holes in the brims of their hats and stuck the long pipes through them whenever they marched, proudly, in the streets, much to their wealthier neighbors' dismay and disapproval.

Characteristic of the English clay is a tilted bowl fitted with a small spur on its bottom, or foot as it is called. The clay, of course, is a direct descendant of the tube pipe, and it is this that accounts for the tilted bowl, a phenomenon observed in several tube-pipe specimens collected in America. The spur, however, is purely an English innovation, and apart from its decorative effect it had three important functions. One of the imperfections of the clay pipe is that it heats up too readily, the bowl becoming unbearable to touch after a short time. The spur, then, acts as a handle of sorts, something on to which the smoker can hold as he puffs. Secondly, if the spur has a flat bottom, as is frequently the case, then the pipe can be rested on a table in an upright position, thus avoiding an embarrassing dumping of ashes over one's wife's best linen cloth. Furthermore, because the hot bowl might be readily cracked if set down on a cold surface, the flat spur allows it to remain in an atmosphere congenial to its future existence. Finally, because the pipe-maker's craft was rightly deemed one of the fine arts, the heel of the spur served as the place whereupon its author could inscribe his mark, something like the title page of a book. Five of these marks, or seals as they are properly called, are illustrated.

Today, due largely to the pre-eminence of the briar burl, clay pipe makers would be destined for extinction were it not for the novelty market. In all of England, there remain but a handful of artisans who rely upon the clay pipe for a living. On the other hand, there is a small coterie of pipe smokers in whose discerning opinion the clay ranks as a pipe without parallel. These few connoisseurs, together with those smokers who want an occasional change from their old stand by or something unique to display among their collection, have kept a very limited number of clay pipe makers in business in recent years.

Suitable pipe clay can be found in nearly all corners of the globe, but for the English, that from Dorsetshire was considered the most desirable. A white plastic clay, when mixed with water it produces a substance whose consistency is not unlike that of putty.

Five Seals of Famous Clay Pipe Manufacturers

This is then siezed and, after much kneading and pounding, rolled into long thin cylinders, each approximating the size and shape of one pipe. Into one end of it is introduced a metal rod, thus causing a passageway that shall become the smoke hole through the stem. The clay is then pressed in a machine such as is illustrated and denoted by the letter A. The excess clay, at this squeezing, is trimmed from the sides and at point f. Machine A is then delivered into the jaws of machine B and, in this manner, protuberance e, being forced down by lever d, hollows out the bowl. The metal rod is then withdrawn from the stem and the pipe is rough-finished. Once the pipe has been deftly trimmed a second time, it is then fired in the kiln until the clay is brittle-hard. Finally, the tips of the stems will be coated with a red wax to prevent the smoker's moist lips from adhering to the dry clay.

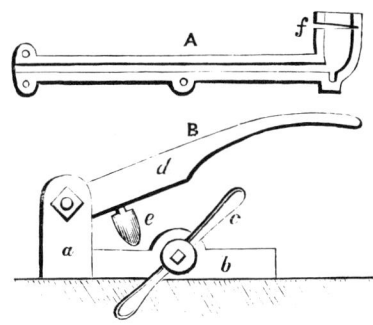

A Machine for Stamping Out Clay Pipes

As previsouly, though casually, remarked, there remains to this day an enlightened segment of the pipe-smoking world that insists upon the clay's unfailing superiority. Their argument rests not so much on Good Old Tradition, but upon the practical and pleasurable aspects of the art. For one thing, clay is a material whose porosity permits it to

Some Curious French Clays

literally drink up the foul and unappetizing moisture that tobacco will frequently exude in combustion. Consequently, the clay pipe yields an exceptionally dry smoke; if this is to your liking, then a clay pipe might well be just what you're looking for. Too, its enthusiasts advance, there is a certain unspoiled earthiness about the pipe that prods pristine feelings to life. The marriage of earth (clay) and plant (tobacco) by fire, some say, is what creates this altogether pleasurable feeling of well-being. Moreover, the American Indians, who knew and cherished pipes like no other race of men, frequently demanded quantities of clay pipes in their barterings with the white man. In exchange for a sizable tract of Pennsylvania, for example, William Penn's remuneration included three hundred pipes of English clay.

The English, however, were not the exclusive manufacturers of clays for use at home and for trade. Departing from the conventional English pattern, it was the French who ultimately emerged as the finest and most imaginative clay pipe makers. The famous

artist M. Gambier and the fine craftsman M. Fiolet, several of whose creations are illustrated, led the field for many decades, using the heads of Napoleon, Rubens, Cavaignac, Hugo, and others for their pipe bowls. Other popular themes included Death, Liberty, Sin, etc., thus catering to everyone's disposition. One pipe, designed by Fiolet, went so far as to depict a scene out of the universally celebrated novel, *Uncle Tom's Cabin*.

Fiolet's Uncle Tom's Cabin

Balancing tobacco pipes was a novel feat introduced for London's amusement: in 1743 a Turk named Mahommed Caratha performed on the slack-rope at Sadler's Wells, firing pistols from each hand as he stood upon it, and balancing at the same time seven tobacco pipes on a ring held in his mouth.
—From Fairholt's Tobacco: Its History and Associations

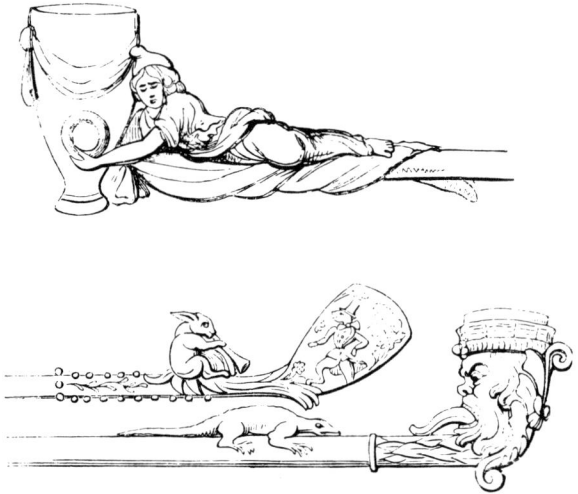

72

Cherrywood

Inevitably, when a civil chat among friends having to do with the pros and cons of various pipes broaches the delicate subject of cherrywood, the issue is hotly contended. Our host, a man whose high opinion of the pipe is only surpassed by his willingness to express it, suggests that anyone who has not enough good sense to recognize its superior qualities ought to be declared legally cracked. Some other gentleman, fairly twitching with rage, retorted that the wood of the cherry tree is no more suitable for the pipe than a sack of wheat flour. At this point in the conversation, several others join in, each entering his own plea with unfettered animosity toward those who oppose him, and what was to have been a cheery evening around the hearth rapidly collapses into a full-fledged brouhaha.

So we get our first fleeting glimpse into the subject at hand and proceed with cautious trepidation. But what is the kernel of this controversy? In a word, taste. Because the wild cherry tree, whence the pipe hails, has about it a quality that drives some people from it like a hive full of hungry hornets and attracts others like a moth to light, it has taken its place as the love-it-or-leave-it of pipes. Possessing the fullest natural bouquet of all pipes, the cherrywood is unmistakably aromatic: even when unlit, it almost perfumes the air. Consequently, when first you stoke it up, the smoke takes on an ebulliency you might previously have thought impossible. Slightly reminiscent of the sweet smell of spring in the arbor, it imparts to your smoking experience a totally new dimension.

And the taste is similarly affected, being lighter and more suggestive than pronounced. There are folks, of course, who do not care for spring in the arbor, at least not in their pipes—those who'd rather sniff the acorn air of late autumn. For these folks the cherrywood can only be a casual acquaintance. If, on the other hand, you relish a more jubilant smoke, then the cherrywood must occupy a prominent slot in your pipe rack.

How to make a Cherrywood pipe

To make a cherrywood pipe, it is first necessary to set forth into the woods, or your neighbor's orchard, and find a cherry tree. (See illustration.) Once you've sighted said tree, locate a fork that looks like any of the drawings in Figure 1. The dimensions of the pipe will be left to your own discrimination. Cherrywoods are very versatile, ranging anywhere from three inches to three feet in length. Bowls a full six inches in diameter I have seen in the shops of London pipe merchants. There is, however, one criterion: The walls of the bowl should be at least half an inch thick. If, as is recommended, you bore a three-quarter-inch tobacco hole, then the smallest overall diameter of the bowl is one and three quarter inches.

The length of the shank is another matter to consider. At the time of cutting, there are two things that must be decided. One is if the pipe is to have an ebonite stem or not. It is quite possible to simply leave a natural wooden stem and bit for the pipe, hand carving it to whatever shape you prefer. Or, you might like to add an ebonite stem and bit, such as are used on briar pipes. This has the

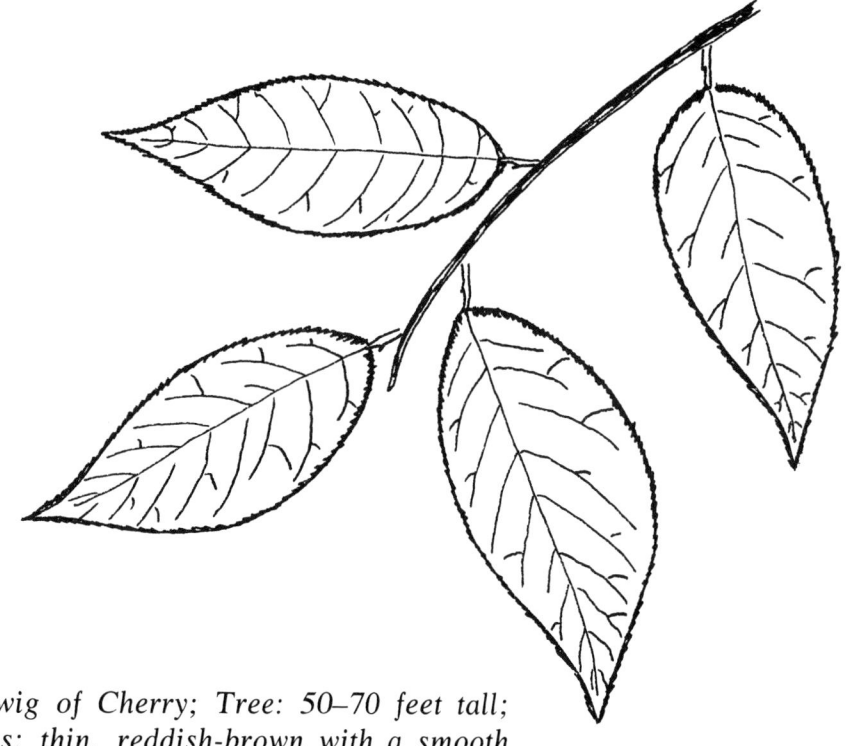

A Twig of Cherry; Tree: 50–70 feet tall; Twigs: thin, reddish-brown with a smooth bark; Leaves: 3–4 inches long, dark green on top, pale green below

advantage of being more hygienic; today, all cherrywoods that are sold on the market are fitted with ebonite stems. So, if you choose the former style, make sure that you cut the fork so that there is enough wood to make a full-sized stem; three to four inches is generally enough. On the other hand, if you plan on fitting your pipe with the additional stem, then about a two-inch shank is adequate. If you elect to add the ebonite stem, you also have the option of a curved stem, but this must be taken into account at cutting time. The general rule to follow is that for a curved stem the shank must meet the bowl at a sixty-degree angle or less. Therefore, according to Figure 1, forks b and c could

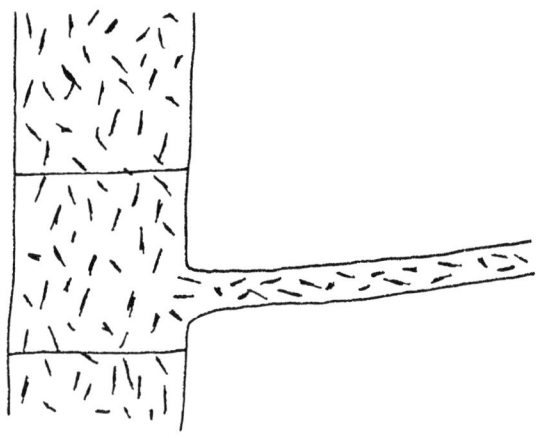

Figure 1a

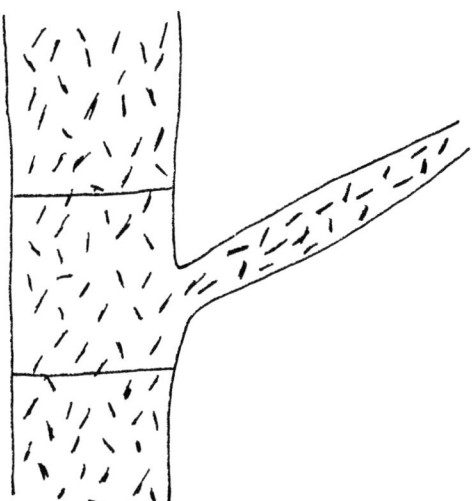

Figure 1b

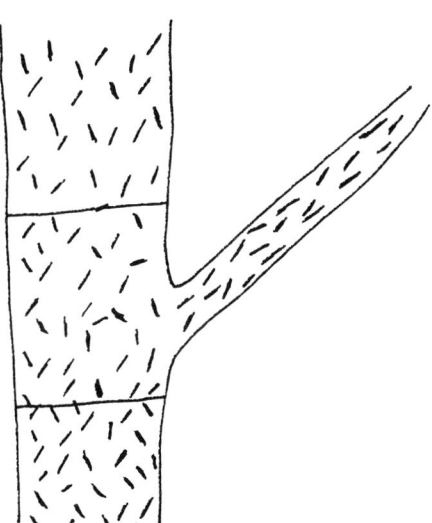

Figure 1c

feasibly accommodate a curved stem, whereas a certainly could not.

After you have cut the forked section, do not be tempted into fiddling with the wood's finish in any way. Leave the bark intact and do not apply any varnish, shellac, or, heaven forbid, paint. The wood of the cherry tree is not so heat-resistant as some of the other pipe woods, notably briar. That is why we have to allow such thick walls all around. But the bark also has an important part to play in the pipe's heating and cooling system; it distributes the heat generated from the center of the bowl evenly over the surface of the pipe and, to a considerable degree, lets the pipe breathe more fully than any finished surface would admit to. It is part of the reason for the cherrywood's reputation as an extremely cool-smoking pipe. Besides, leaving the bark intact enhances its rustic charm and has been characteristic of the pipe ever since it was first made.

Once a fine sturdy fork has been cut, it is next to devise a special bowl-cutting bit from an ordinary wood-boring bit. Following the drawing in Figure 2, file down the bit until its bottom cutting edge is nicely rounded. This same bit can also be used for other pipes, briar included. After this has been done, you can proceed with the boring of the tobacco hole. To start the hole, drill down about a half inch with a quarter-inch twist drill in the exact center of what will become the bowl: This will provide a niche into which the rounded edge of the bit can burrow accurately. When drilling, remember to leave as much thickness at the base, or foot, of the pipe as you did for the walls. (See Figure 3.)

To drill the smoke hole, as in Figure 4, use an eighth-inch twist drill, making the hole as true as possible. At this point, the tip of the stem can be carved down to shape the

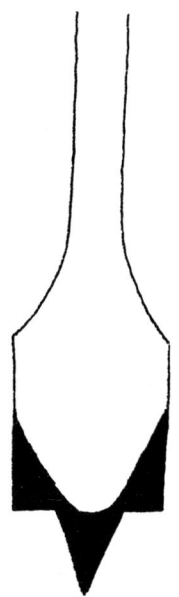

Figure 2

Instructions for adding an ebonite stem, curved or otherwise, are given in full detail in the section on briar pipe making in this chapter. The same procedure is applicable for both the cherrywood and the briar pipe.

Whether you have chosen a plain wooden stem or one of ebonite, you might want to contour the foot of the pipe so that it sits comfortably in your hand. A flat file, to grind down the edges, followed by some sandpapering, is enough to achieve the desired effect. (See Figure 6.) Do not remove any bark from the walls of the bowl; a touch of carnauba wax rubbed into the bottom will in no way affect the heating system and will most definitely enhance the pipe's appearance and feel.

Because your cherrywood has not been artificially dried or seasoned, it is up to you to do so properly. Begin by smoking a full bowl of very loosely packed tobacco and repeat this operation several times, letting the bowl cool thoroughly between smokes. As a char builds up on the interior walls, the amount of tobacco should be gradually increased. By using this process, you actually "smoke" the bowl dry, curing it like sugar ham and thus producing a cool, sweet pipe.

bit, if you have elected for the all-wood stem. To do so, use a sharp woodcarving knife. Note that toward the end (see Figure 5), the stem flattens out a bit, taking on an ovalness, then flairs out to provide the traditional mouthpiece. Other possibilities exist, of course, and the reader is invited to use his imagination.

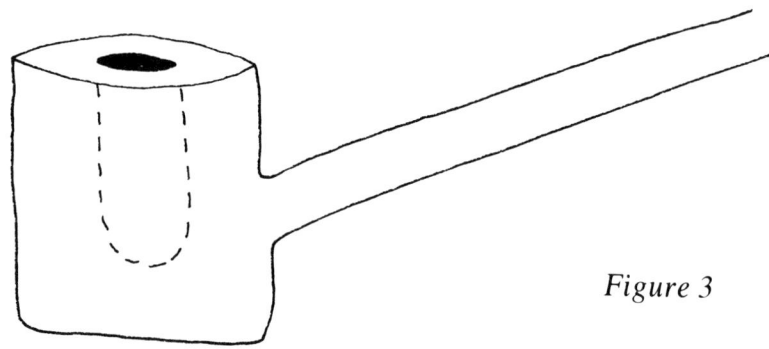

Figure 3

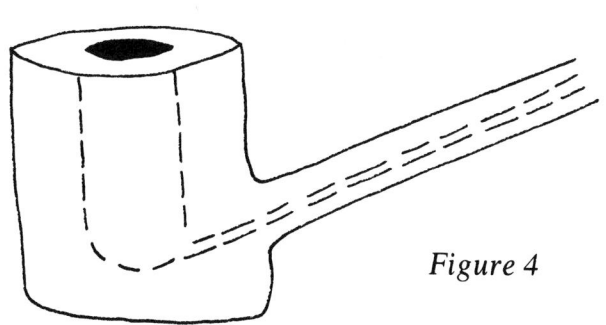

Figure 4

Figure 5

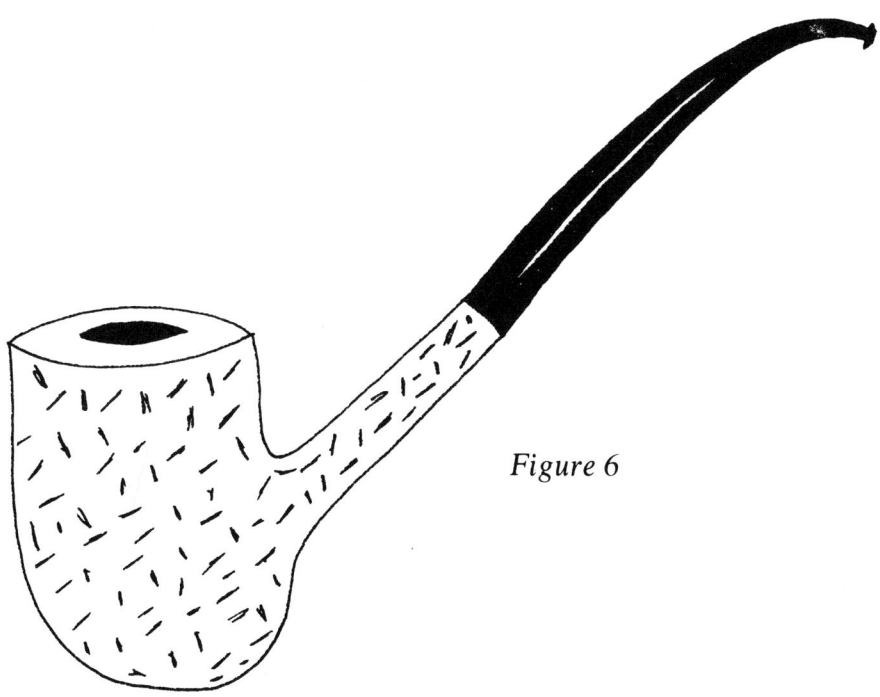

Figure 6

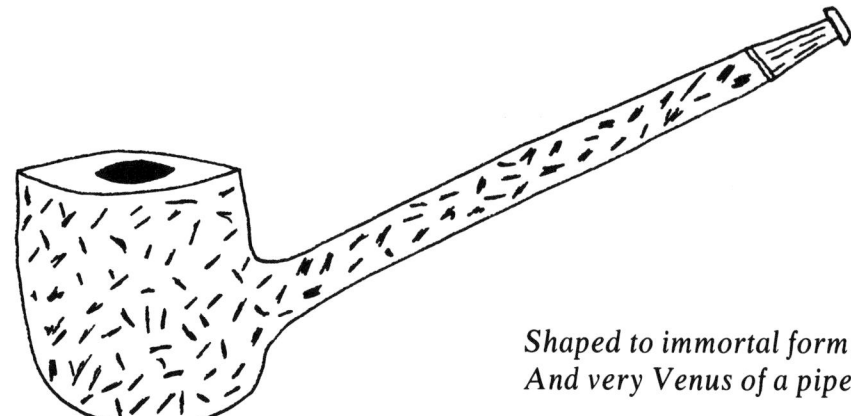

*Shaped to immortal form, the type
And very Venus of a pipe.*

—From James Russell Lowell's
On the Gift of a Meerschaum Pipe

Figure 6 (continued)

Meerschaum

*A meerschaum pure, t' would float as light
As she the girls call Amphitrite.
Mixture divine of foam and clay,
From both it stole the best away;
Its foam is such as crowns the glow
Of breakers brimmed by Veuve Clicquot;
Its clay is but congested lymph
Jove chose to make some choicer nymph;
And her combined, —why, this must be
The birth of some enchanted sea,*

In the private smoking clubs that proliferated in the nineteenth century where, it should be mentioned at the onset, its members were very fussy about their pipes, the sovereign meerschaum was their acknowledged Queen of Pipes, a title, we might add, she has had no call to renounce. A wondrous compound of silica, magnesia, carbonic acid, and water, meerschaum so resembles petrified sea foam that its original German nomenclators unhesitatingly called it just that: sea foam, or as the French say, *ècume de mer*. Mined primarily in Asia Minor, meerschaum is an extremely lightweight, highly porous material that, when first excavated, can be made to lather like a piece of laundry soap. In fact, soap is precisely what the natives had been using it for prior to the time when its talents could be put to a nobler use.

Like the lady she is, meerschaum first had to be refined before she could be introduced to polite society, and though her existence had been known for many centuries, she

Cutting Off the Clay From Raw Meerschaum Blocks (Hayim Pinhas, Istanbul)

could not be utilized for the pipe until rather recently. In its crude state, it is entirely unserviceable: Due to its delicate nature, it carbonizes so rapidly as to be rendered useless after but a dozen or so smokes. However, thanks to the untiring efforts of some very astute gentlemen (or, as some would have it, sheer accident), since the latter part of the eighteenth century the meerschaum pipe has enjoyed a very praiseworthy reputation indeed.

When meerschaum is first dug from the earth, where it lies embedded in stratas of reddish-brown clay, it is of a most disagreeable appearance, a dirty white lump discolored by blots and blemishes. Immediately, before the unkind air can preserve this tarnished look, it is boiled in milk, which, besides flushing out particles of clay and other debris, imparts to it that magnificent whiteness for which it is so very much admired. Its beauty fully blossomed, the next and all-important step is another bath, this time in hot wax or tallow. Above all, it is this procedure that fortifies the pipe; by seeping deep into the meerschaum's many pores, the hot wax serves to mollify the destructive forces of combustion and so increase the pipe's longevity dramatically. A well-cared-for meerschaum will outlast its owner.

One of the most absorbent of materials, meerschaum was considered a blessing for smokers by many members of the medical profession. Unlike many other substances used for pipes, notably clay, meerschaum will not lose its original composition, thereby endangering the smoker's mouth and

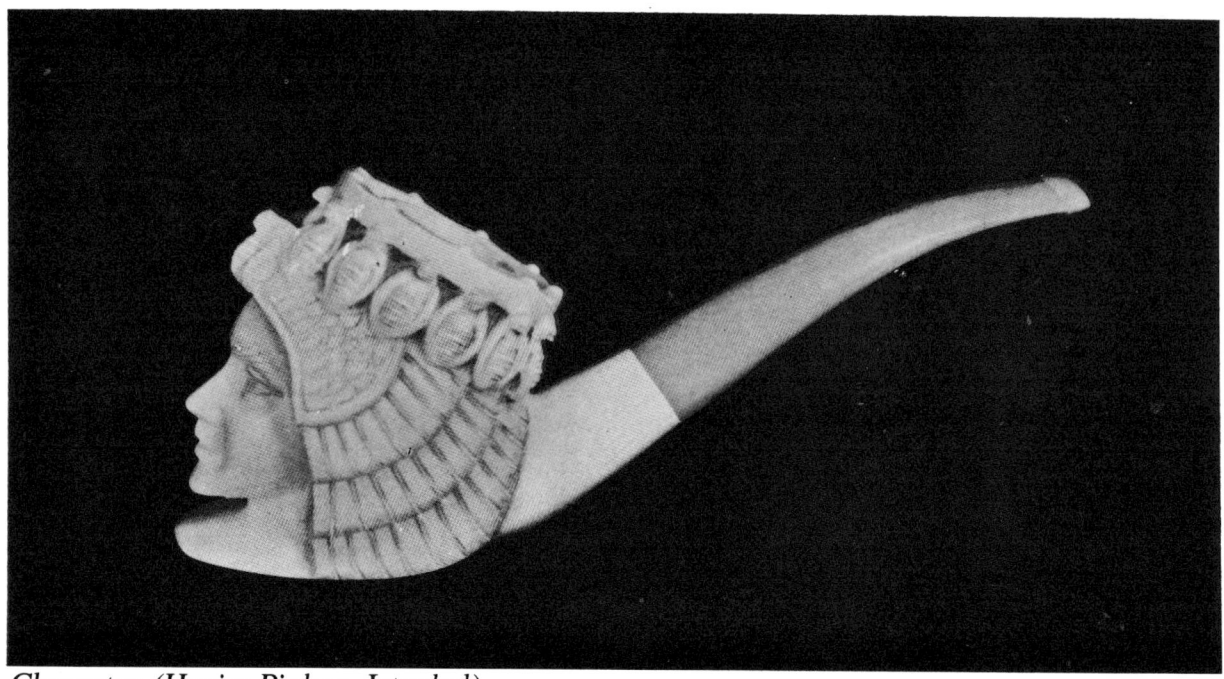

Cleopatra (Hayim Pinhas, Istanbul)

throat with foreign particles. Another and more arresting feature of the meerschaum pipe is its marvelous talent for coloring. When tobacco burns, as any pipe smoker knows, it gives off foul juices that, in ordinary pipes, collect in miserable deposits at the bottom of the bowl, occasionally sneaking up through the stem and spoiling a smoke. But meerschaum pipes have the ability to absorb all those unsavory juices and, what's more, transform them into delectable, ambrosial nectars that enhance the pipe's flavor and aroma infinitely. All the while, as more and more juices are absorbed, the entire pipe colors, ranging from a rich golden hue, after the first couple of bowlfuls, to a handsome mahogany after several years of steady smoking.

Coloring meerschaums has become one of the pipeman's foremost preoccupations, and extreme examples of this are cited throughout smoking literature. One immoderate fellow, an Englishman of high army rank, once enlisted an entire regiment for this purpose. Knowing that the ultimate in coloration could only be achieved if the pipe, once lit, was not permitted to cool, he had each soldier, in turn, smoke his meerschaum for a full seven months, after which time elapsed he was the possessor of both the world's most perfect pipe as well as a bill for one hundred pounds for the tobacco consumed in this mind-boggling effort. On this subject of coloration, the chatty Oliver Wendell Holmes remarked:

Certain things are good for nothing until they have been kept a long while: and some things are good for nothing until they have been long kept and used. Of the first, wine is the illustrious and immortal example. Of those which must be kept and used I will name three, —meerschaum pipes, violins and po-

ems. The meerschaum is but a poor affair until it has burned a thousand offerings to the cloud-compelling dieties. It comes to us without complexion or flavor, —born of the sea foam, like Aphrodite, but colourless as *pallida Nors* herself. The fire is lighted in its central shrine, and gradually the juices which the broad leaves of the Great Vegetable had sucked up from an acre and curdle into a drachm are diffused through its thirsting pores. First a discoloration, then a stain, and at last a rich, glowing umber tint spreading over the whole surface. Nature true to her old brown autumnal hue, you see, —as true in the fire of the meerschaum as in the sunshine of October! And then the cumulative wealth of its fragrant reminiscences! he who inhales it vapors takes a thousand whiffs in a single breath; and one cannot touch it without awakening the old joys that hang around it as the smell of flowers cling to the dresses of the daughters of the house of Farina!

Certainly she is a lady of engaging charm and bewitching beatitude. But, lest we forget, she is a woman and, this being the case, her temperamental nature cannot be overlooked or sidestepped.

The Meerschaum Fancier's Ten Commandments

1. *Do not* touch the warm bowl with your fingers, as the moisture deposited there will adversely affect the natural coloring.

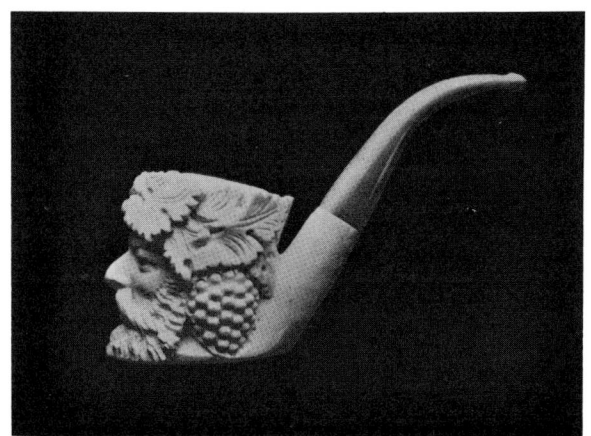

Bacchus (Hayim Pinhas, Istanbul)

2. *Do not* set a warm pipe on a cold surface since this admixture of temperatures may very likely result in a crack or similar disfigurement.

3. *Do not* smoke a meerschaum pipe out of doors as even the most feeble wind will disturb the even coloration.

4. *Do not* clean the inside of a meerschaum pipe until it has cooled to room temperature; nor ever use alcohol or any commerical cleanser on a meerschaum pipe.

5. *Do not*, when cleaning the pipe, use any sharp instruments as these may inadvertently pierce the pipe.

6. *Do* clean the inside of the bowl often to remove the leavings that are not absorbed, and that appear as an unsightly crust.

7. *Do* break in a meerschaum pipe by calculated degrees; that is, begin with a cautious quarter bowlful lightly packed, then, after several smokes like this, increase the dosage to a half and then, but only after twenty smokes, a full bowl.

8. *Do* leave a few shreds of tobacco unburned at the bottom of the bowl at the end of each smoke. Never finish the tobacco to

its ashy end when smoking a meerschaum.

9. *Do* smoke a meerschaum only if it is at room temperature or warmer. Never smoke a chilled pipe, such as one that has been left out of doors on the dashboard of your automobile.

10. *Do* draw your smoke in easily, taking steady and gentle whiffs. This will not only ensure perfect coloration but maintain the pipe's perfect health. *Never treat a meerschaum with hurried indifference, and she will reward you with satisfaction out of the ordinary.*

Being the subject of much versifying and prose writing, the pipe has had interesting literary associations; no pipe, though, has been the subject of such tintinnabulation as the meerschaum, compelling authors everywhere to do her homage. But in one respect particularly does the meerschaum outshine her cousins: It is the only pipe that has had the lead part in a dramatic play. Entitled *Mere Sham*, it is a farcical offering presented to the public in 1875. It involves "a young married man with an inveterate habit of smoking," Harry Ingham, and his wife's, Estelle's, campaign to put an end to Harry's habit. After some bickering, Harry relents and agrees to give up the pipe; Estelle is fairly thrilled at the prospect. Later on that week, however, Harry discovers that his love for the weed that he cannot have is swiftly replacing his love for his wife. He becomes miserable with worry but dares not resume the habit he has sworn off lest his wife and friends think him a weak-willed bounder. So . . . he enlists the aid of his friend, Stephen, and together they arrive at the solution. Stephen, who is conveniently a doctor, will administer "a dose of hasheesh" to Harry; in turn, Harry will act insane and, by his actions, convince Estelle to willfully "restore his pipes." The following scene, the triumphant climax of the play, depicts Stephen and Estelle watching Harry act out his artful machination.

ESTELLE	*(grasping STEPHEN'S arm with a look of horror.) Oh Stephen! He is out of his mind! What is it?*
STEPHEN	*Keep perfectly quiet, Estelle. I've seen cases like this before. It is only a temporary affection. . . . (pouring her a glass of wine —HARRY meantime . . . mounts the library table, and lies upon it—face down. Raises his head and supports it with both hands under the chin—then raises his feet, thus presenting the figure of a monster meerschaum).*
STEPHEN	*He imagines himself to be a meerschaum. Let him alone —he will do no harm.*
HARRY	*Am I coloring well?*
STEPHEN	*Capitally!*
HARRY	*. . . Did you ever see a finer mahogany hue?*

After a bit more of this treatment, Estelle is quite persuaded that Harry's insanity was induced by her foolish whim that he quit smoking, and, with apologies, she invites her restored husband into the smoking room where his pipes and tobacco await his pleasure.

Briar

It was in the post-Napoleonic 1820s that a chance incident on the isle of Corsica transformed the pipe industry so radically that its effects are manifest to this day. Visiting that hot and sea-struck isle was a French pipe maker; being himself a voracious smoker, he brought along one of his finest and best-loved meerschaums. Upon his arrival, however, he accidentally dropped his beloved pipe; it cracked most irreparably, and there he was, hundreds of miles from home with no pipe to smoke. But in one of the isle's tiny villages, he heard, lived an old mountain man who reputably could perform wonders with a woodcarving knife, and so, with all haste, he invited the carver to make him a pipe from whatever local material he thought best. He then left the man to his work and waited impatiently for his pipe at the hotel. When the new pipe was at last ready, the old man presented it to the Frenchman. Being of the meerschaum school, and at that time that was *the* school to belong to, he was not overly enthusiastic—at first; indeed, he had seen and smoked pipes of wood before and could not particularly see any future for them. Still, it was a handsome pipe, and he lit it up. Well, it didn't take but a couple of bowls and the pipe maker had turned his thinking around dramatically: here was a pipe, he thought, that had great potential, and he took it and several other samples of the wood back to France and his studio.

Within twenty-five years, this type of pipe had brought ruin to the clay, deflated the sovereign meerschaum, and become the object of universal praise and acceptance. It was, of course, the briar pipe.

The briar burl, the hard knotty part of the heath tree whence the pipe derives, is found principally in those countries that border the Mediterranean Sea. There the climate is altogether unsuitable for plant life: The soil is sandy and rocky, there is a scant minimum of rainfall, and high winds incessantely and mercilessly test the plants' endurance. These unfavorable conditions, however, are necessary to the production of good sturdy burls. For the heath tree (*Erica Arborea* in botanical nomenclature, *bruyere* in French), in its constant struggle for survival, produces the burl so that it can persevere. Located at the junction of the roots and the trunk, the burl is a tightly knit knob of wood that acts both as a root terminal and to hold the tree fast when the heavy winds roar. Due to its dual nature, it must be both large enough to send down a network of roots and strong enough to secure the twenty-foot-high tree under brutal winds.

But in order for the burl to attain maturity and, subsequently, be of sufficient size and dense enough consistency for the pipe, it takes anywhere from sixty to two hundred years. The older the burl the better the chance that it can yield perhaps a score of flawless pipes. However, not all burls of sufficient size are satisfactory. For on the burl's long and tedious road to adulthood, it frequently encounters a pebble, a piece of debris, or even a dead insect. What happens when it meets such an object is that the burl then grows, amoeba-like, around the obstruction, and so incorporates it into its mass. Consequently, a large number of burls contain imperfections. If foreign matter is too prevalent in the burl or if there are but one or two encapsulations too near the heart of it, the entire burl may have to be discarded and a hundred or more years of laborious growth come to naught.

It is precisely for this reason that some

Selecting and Weighing Choice Burls   (Courtesy of Alfred Dunhill of London Limited)

pipe manufacturers have recently taken to the malpractice of using inferior portions of the burl to stretch the profit. These portions generally come from the "branch," one of the larger roots growing out of the burl proper. In these instances, the briar is not as close-grained as it ought to be. In turn, this makes an altogether inferior pipe, more likely to give dissatisfaction than not. Whether you are selecting an unfinished block or a finished pipe, therefore, it is of utmost importance to be certain that what you are purchasing has been cut from the interior sphere of the burl itself, marked by its close-grained and unflawed texture. Reputable makers and merchants, it might be added, can generally be trusted to point out any existing imperfections in their products, inferior briar included.

Still, there exists a sufficient supply of good briar (coming from Spain, Algeria, Sicily, Greece, Sardinia, and other countries that touch the Sea) to elevate the briar pipe to a position once held by the clay; that is, Everyman's pipe. For today, when a gentleman makes reference to his pipe, tender or otherwise, chances are excellent that it is a briar. We know it is popular, overwhelmingly so: What then is it appeal? In all modesty, the briar has an amalgam of fine qualities that the clay, and for that matter the meerschaum, could never approach. To begin with the most obvious, both the clay and the meerschaum are notorious for their fragility. One drop to the floor and they are gone forever. Drop a briar to the floor, however, and ninety-nine times out of a hundred it will bounce back in chipper spirits.

The briar burl, due to its tenuous mountain existence, becomes hard, it is true, but surprisingly not callous; in this happy phenomenon lies its special appeal. For one thing, the obdurate hardness of the burl makes the pipe very nearly shock-proff; too, and just as vital, it causes the pipe to be adequately fire-resistant. Not perfectly resistant to a forest fire or one of that magnitude, the pipe does resist most of the ill effects of combustion, and, what it cannot resist, it uses to highly efficacious ends. Heat, of course, is the inevitable result of the tobacco's combustion. In some pipes this heat is effectively generated right to the outside of the pipe; consequently, you feel like you're holding the business end of a branding iron instead of your pipe. But the briar, in its wondrous way, uses that heat in such a fashion as to ultimately seduce the tobacco into

The Professional Way: From Burl to Briar Pipe
(Courtesy of Alfred Dunhill of London, Limited)

yielding its fullest taste and fragrance.

It is a felicitous fact that as the tobacco burns, a scorchingly intimate relationship between it and the briar blossoms, so intimate in fact that it produces an offspring. For in burning, the tobacco generates an intense and concentrated heat; this heat then causes the interior walls of the bowl to expand: but, being a very closegrained wood, the briar expands only slightly, not too much so as to deliver the heat directly to your hand, not too little so as not to admit any of the moisture (which is concomitant with the heat). It is, as previously stated, adequately, not perfectly, fire-resistant. So, in its expansion, the briar accepts the volatile essences and oils of the tobacco at a miserly rate. When the pipe cools and the briar contracts, the tobacco essence and the wood have formed an inseparable union, a marriage if you will. And, unselfishly merging their separate identities, they each contribute to produce a third. Like a son, this new creation is harder than either of the parents, and like a daughter more sensitive; the "love child," it is properly called the char.

Once this primary char has been produced, say after a dozen or so smokes, it then serves as the foundation for the secondary char, or what we might refer to as the char proper. Constructed largely by the hot toils of the tobacco, the char will steadily accumulate and thicken in direct proportion to the number of bowlfuls smoked, and, if left to itself, will one day take over the entire bowl; this, though, is certainly not the desired effect, and therefore a reamer must be periodically employed to maintain the char's thickness at one-sixteenth of an inch. This matter of reaming will be considered more fully later.

It is this special property of the briar, then, that is applauded so heartily. It is this property that lends to the pipe its subdued air of titillation that can be so sensibly heady. For as the worthy weed is consumed, the smoke passes now in now out of the char, much as Alice slipped through the looking glass only to discover a marvelous and previously hidden world. In like manner does the smoke, which curls up to you direct from re-entry as it were, reveal similar unimaginable pleasures to you, its conjurer. And as Wonderland itself took on a different feeling at each corner, so, too, does the briar yield a myriad of delights in its never-ending process of maturation, concentrating as it does so well more and more and still more of the tobacco's bright but secret heart.

How to make a briar pipe

To make a briar pipe that is both a beautiful piece of hand-hewn craftsmanship as well as a fine smoking pipe, it is essential to begin with the finest of materials. Briar blocks (see Figure 1), preseasoned, can be purchased either at a pipe shop or direct from a dealer in pipe parts. In any good-sized city there is bound to be at least one large pipe shop, and usually they'll carry briar blocks, if not a complete line at least a modest selection. Otherwise, you'll have to locate either a pipe-repair shop or a parts dealer in your area. If you wish to order by mail, a reputable merchant is J. H. Lowe (Box A74, Wantagh, New York 11793). Upon request, he'll send you a free catalogue in which can be found thousands of different stems as well as briar blocks of varying dimensions. If, however, you have the opportunity to select your block personally, watch out for the one that appears to be the most closely grained, this being the tightest, hardest, and best. Generally, the blocks will be a sort of rich honey color, this being their natural color. Prestained blocks should be avoided. Recently, as many briar fields have become exhausted due to the ever-increasing demand for pipes, the prices of unworked blocks has increased. Still, for a couple of dollars you can buy a first-quality block of aged briar.

At the same time a block is purchased, a suitable stem should be selected. Made of ebonite (very hard vulcanized rubber), these stems will not be affected by moisture for perhaps ten years, and they add no taste of their own. These stems can often be found at the same places where blocks are sold, though quite frequently a large assortment of stems will be found in a pipe shop even though that same shop carries no blocks. Pipe-shop owners like to keep a good quantity on hand for repairs and replacements of very old stems that are beginning to show their age.

Ebonite stems come in a wide variety of shapes and sizes. (See Figure 2.) When selecting a stem, you must take into consideration the style you want your pipe to be. Is it to be a long-shanked Canadian, a Bent, a Lovat, an Oom-Paul, a Prince, a Bulldog? (See Figure 3.) As you can see, the briar "pipe" and the ebonite stem must be coordinated. (Note that when you purchase the stem, it will almost invariably be straight. Bending the stem is something we must do ourselves, and this will be discussed later. Also, the stem will probably not come with a tenon, that is the smaller extended part that fits into the briar. This, too, must be fashioned by hand and will be taken up at the appropriate time.)

The first operation is to drill the tobacco

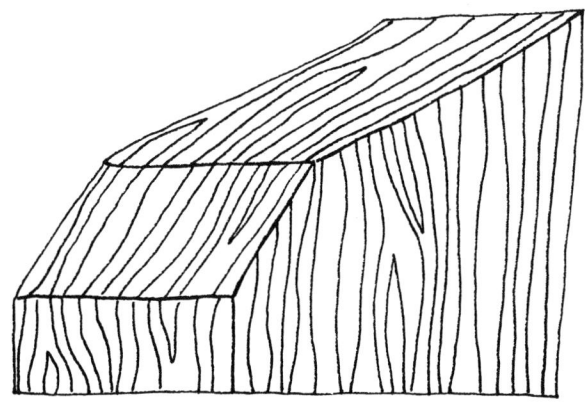

Figure 1

hole in the top of the block. The bit to use is a modified wood-boring bit. (See Figure 4.) This rounded bit is made by filing off the sharp edges until it is rounded and smooth. Generally speaking, a three-quarter-inch bit should be used, but for certain styles a smaller or larger bit may be necessary. The hole should be drilled as indicated in Figure 5, leaving at least a half inch all around. This excess will later be trimmed off as the pipe is shaped to its final dimensions. To start the rounded bit, it is a good idea to first drill a small hole (quarter inch) in the exact center of what will become your bowl. In this way the rounded edge will not "run" all over the top of the block before catching.

Our next job is to drill the smoke hole. A one-eighth-inch twist drill does this nicely. In order to determine the precise place to begin the drilling, follow this rule: Subtract the depth of the tobacco hole from the overall height of the block; this distance, generally a fraction of an inch, is then the height at which the smoke hole should be drilled at the other end of the block. For example (see Figure 5A), if the overall height of the block is two inches and the depth of the tobacco hole (the bowl) is one

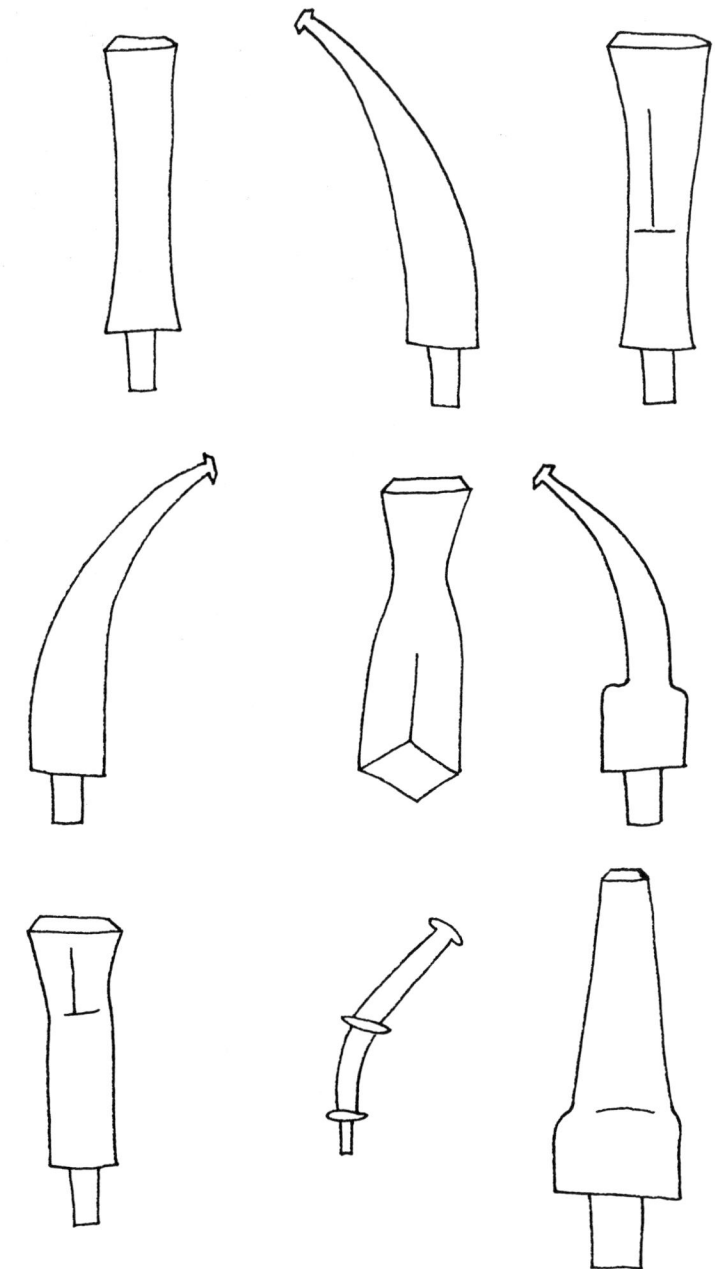

Figure 2

and a half inches, then the smoke hole should be drilled at a height of one-half inch. (See arrow.) This calculation is to ensure that the smoke hole will meet the bowl right at its very bottom and not somewhere too high in the bowl or even below it. Consequently, this hole must be drilled carefully, aiming for a true ninety-degree angle. For the curved pipe (see Figure 5B), the procedure is basically the same except that the smoke hole must be drilled from the slanting plane of the block.

Then change the bit in your drill to a quarter-inch twist drill and bore out the tenon hole. This operation is really nothing more than enlarging the end of the smoke hole so that the stem's tenon will be able to slide into it. The tenon hole should be about three-quarters of an inch deep. (See Figure 6.)

Once the tenon hole has been bored, it is next to make the tenon so that it fits snugly inside it. To do this, clamp your drill sideways in the vise and equip it with a bit that screws tightly into the hole in the stem. (See Figure 7.) This then serves as a makeshift lathe and is perfect for our purpose. Click the drill on and lock it on with the tiny button on the handle. Then, using a flat file, shape the tenon until it fits tightly into the hole you have made for it. (i.e., the diameter of the tenon should be a uniform quarter inch or just ever so slightly less than that.) The turning of the tenon demands a light touch with the file; this is a delicate operation and should be undertaken with great pains to ensure a proper fit. Be careful not to take too much off too fast since if the tenon is too small the entire stem has to be discarded; therefore, work slowly and remember that the fit should be exquisitely snug. In determining the length of the tenon, make it just a little shorter than the depth of the tenon

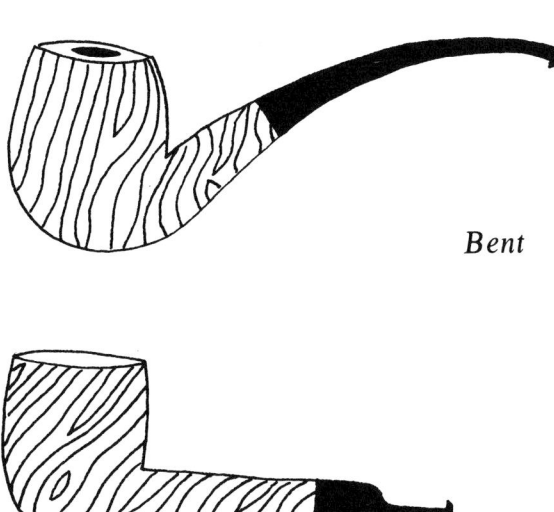

Bent

Lovat

Bulldog

Figure 3

hole—a sixteenth-inch discrepancy is fine.

Once all the holes have been bored and the tenon made and fitted, the actual shaping process can begin. Start by cutting away excess block as indicated in Figure 8. Briar is a very hard wood, as you have undoubtedly discovered, and this precludes the use of an ordinary wood saw. Instead, a hacksaw must be used to make these and all subsequent cuts. Before cutting, it is good policy to scribe the lines on the block with a mark-

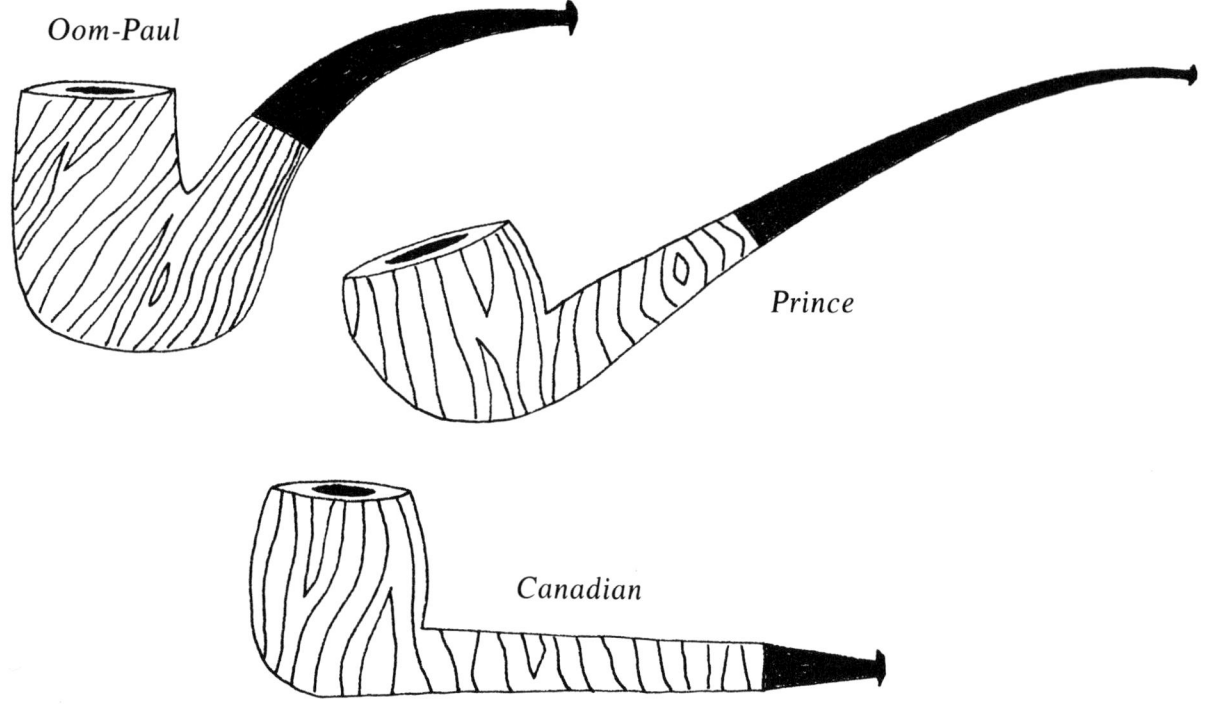

Figure 3 (continued)

ing crayon and a straight edge.

Cuts on the shank portion should be made next. (See Figure 9.) These cuts should not take off so much that the shank diameter is now smaller than the stem; in fact the shank should be larger all around.

Next, scribe four diagonal lines on the top of the block (see Figure 10) and cut away the excess. At this point, the pipe should begin to take on a familiar shape. (See Figure 11A and B.)

Before proceeding with the finishing, now is a good time to curve the stem, if that's what your plans call for. Ebonite, being a variety of rubber, will become flexible when held over a steam bath or even a candle. As the rubber begins to soften, gently curve the stem to the position desired. If you're using a

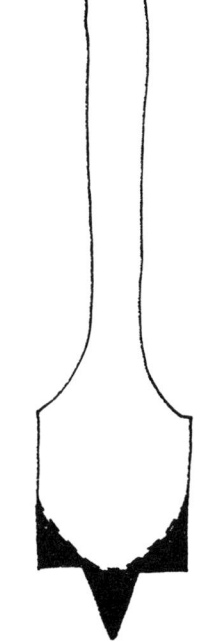

Figure 4

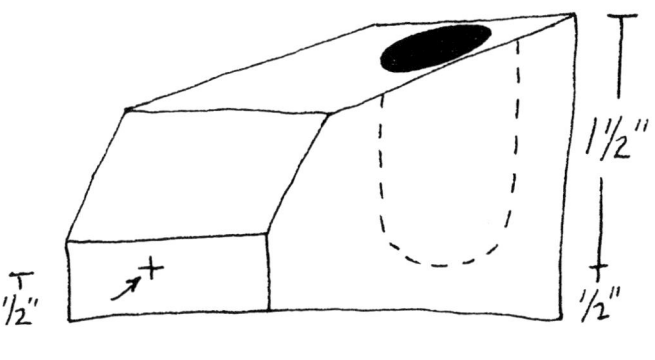

Figure 5a

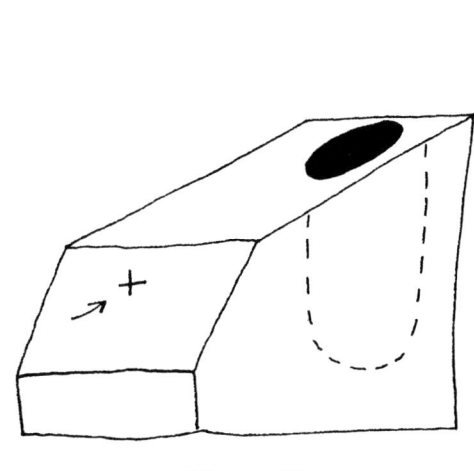

Figure 5b

candle, be sure to hold the stem far enough from the flame (no less than three inches) so that it won't begin to burn. Also, while heating the stem, try to soften a fairly large area, otherwise the stem tends to fold over just at one point and doesn't take on that nice graceful sweep that so handsomely compliments the pipe. Be sure to allow the stem time to cool thoroughly before fitting it back into the pipe.

The pipe is now ready for its final shaping. Begin this process by using a coarse file, working slowly to attain a perfectly symmetrical bowl and shank. The shank should now be filed down to nearly the level of the stem. It is a good idea not to file away any of the ebonite at this time. Later, if you find it necessary, a little sandpaper will suffice. As the pipe begins to take shape, switch to a finer file. For the area at the junction of the bowl and shank, use a rattail file to achieve a nicely curved meeting. When you have laid the files aside for the last time, the pipe should be the exact shape you want it to be.

The pipe will undoubtedly be covered with file scratches; this unavoidable. However, they really must be done away with if the pipe is to have a polished professional look and feel. Have on hand coarse, medium, and fine (extra-fine, too) sandpaper and

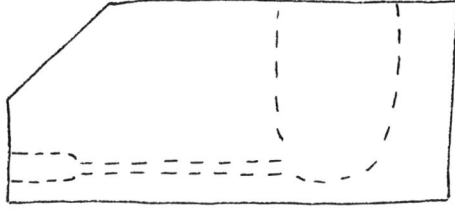

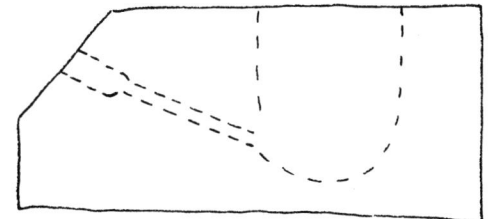

Figure 6

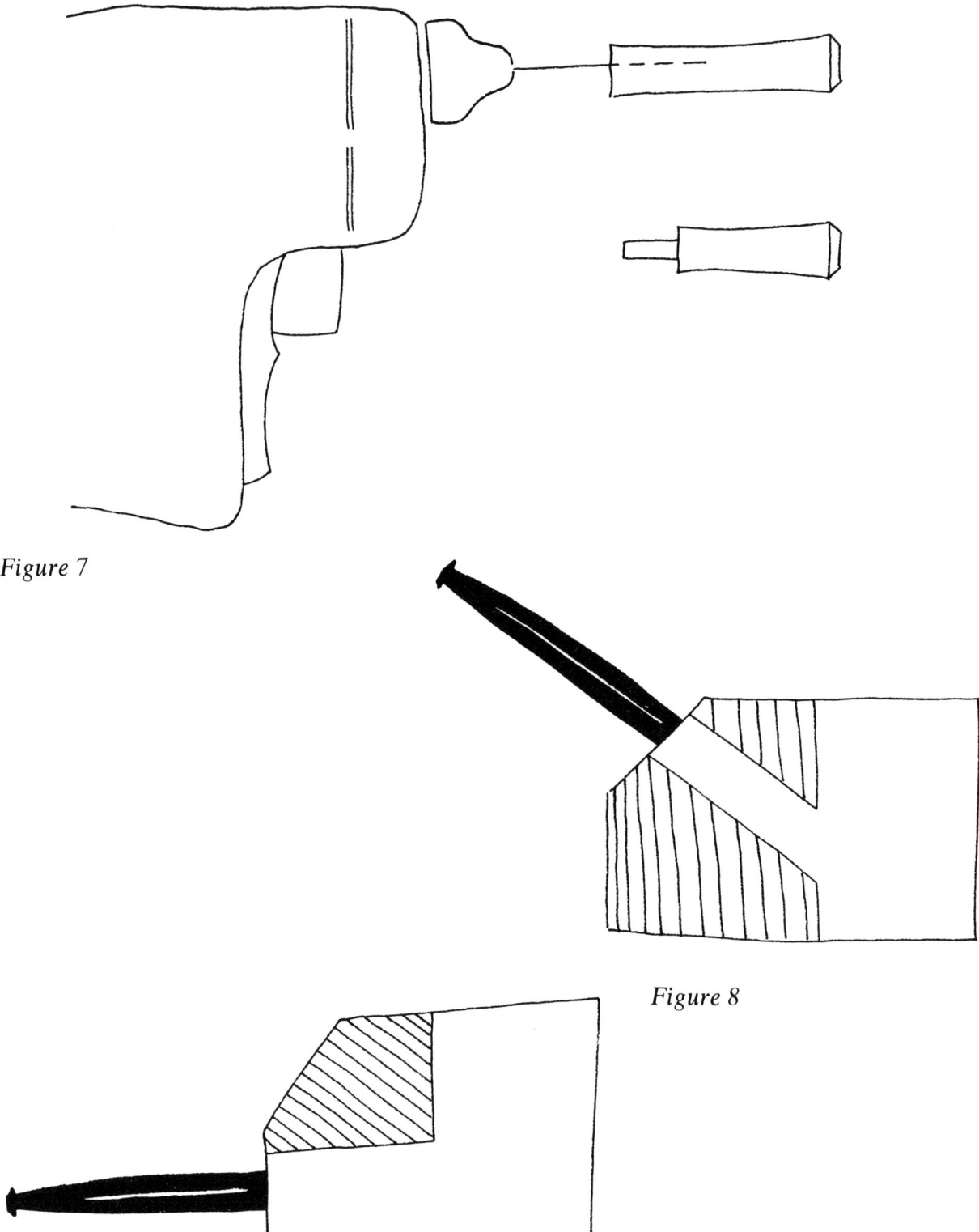

Figure 7

Figure 8

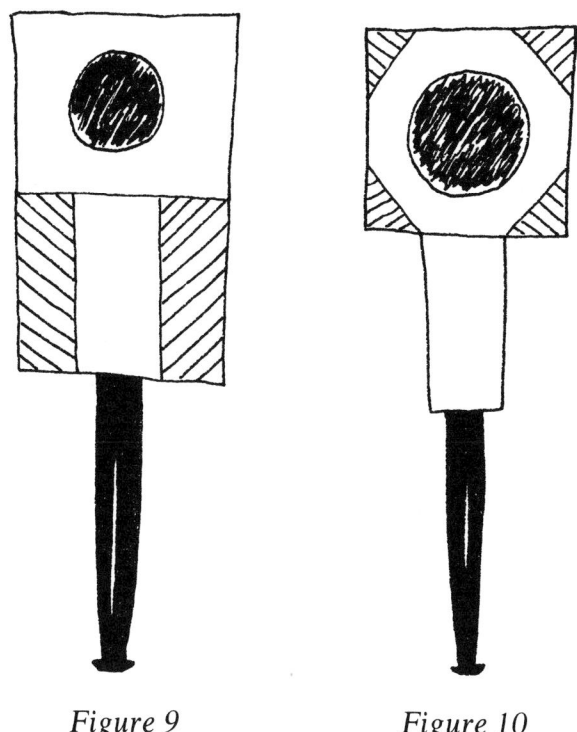

Figure 9 *Figure 10*

today are polished with a special compound called tripoli. This is a very high-quality polish and is used not only by pipe makers but by jewelers as well. Sold in blocks, the tripoli compound should be applied to the buffing disc, the drill engaged, and the polishing can commence. Polish all areas of the pipe, stem included.

Once the pipe has been stained and polished, it should be waxed to bring out and preserve the highlights of the wood. Carnauba wax is the acknowledged best, and it should be administered generously in the same manner as the tripoli, using, of course, a fresh buffing disc.

The finished pipe before you, there is nothing left but to light it up and reap the unparalleled pleasures of utilizing so delightfully something you made yourself. But, before you admire her in action, here are some tips.

go to work. This is perhaps the most laborious of all the operations, but as the surface begins to smooth out, it is well worth the effort. In sanding, be certain that the stem and shank form one continuous piece —if needed, the ebonite can be sanded. A good polishing later will restore its original gloss.

For the final stages of finishing it is advisable to use a buffing disc. The buffing disc is a soft, clothlike wheel that, when attached to your drill, makes a very effective high-speed polisher and waxer. To finish the pipe in the traditional style, first stain the pipe the color of your choice. This of course is not mandatory, and many people find the natural color attractive and elect to leave it be. If you want to stain, however, I would suggest not staining the inside of the bowl. This only tends to delay the seasoning process.

All briar pipes that you see in the shops

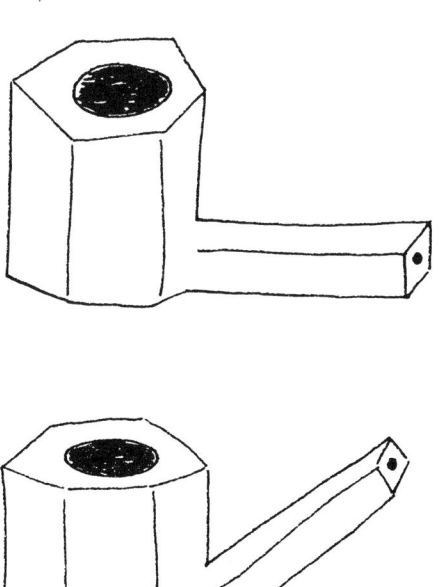

Figure 11

Good things to know (about a briar pipe)

On Breaking In a New Pipe

Was there ever an inveterate smoker of pipes who did not claim to know the one and only correct procedure for breaking in a virgin briar? I think not. Pipe smokers, especially those who have invested considerable lengths of time and amounts of energy to this most worthy of all pastimes, acquire much mysterious knowledge, much of it arcane, about pipes and about other things. But one thing all confirmed pipe smokers profess to know is how to break in a new pipe. For instance, one oldtimer I met in Canada confided to me one day that the only right way to break in a briar was to bury it under some rich loamy soil and leave it be for a period of no less than one month. At the end of said ordeal, the pipe should be excavated and very carefully dusted off. Only then, said he, was it fit for his choicest tobacco. Another method, this suggested by a Parisian pipe dealer, is to fill the bowl of the pipe full to the brim with cask-aged brandy from the cellars of some celebrated distillery and, stepping back to a safe distance, set fire to it. Let it burn freely, he declared, and when the bowl is dry you've broken her in *avec le feu doux*. Other methods I have heard are equally startling but, to my knowledge, as ill-suited as can be.

The briar pipe, despite its rugged looks and strong constitution, possesses a very sensitive soul. Mistreat it at the beginning and it will mistreat you forever. So if you absolutely insist on using brandy, rum, or some other pet alcoholic tonic, do so in the kindest, least injurious manner. A rag or cloth, soaked in said tonic, then swished about gaily inside the bowl, should be sufficient libation for any pipe. Advocates of alcohol claim that it ably prepares the pipe for the initial razzing by fire. This may be true, and if the above procedure is employed, it is at least not damaging. On the other hand, scorching out the insides with a blow torch, using the hapless bowl as a cruet for wine vinegar, and all similarly inane measures are not to be tolerated.

We now arrive at the all-important moment: the first smoke. And if the pipe is to be broken in satisfactorily (satisfactorily here defined as that singular way that will impart to you pleasure unending and unfathomable), it has to be with the patience for which pipe smokers are so renowned. So . . . for the first five (5) smokes, you must fill the bowl but a quarter full, and at that the tobacco ought to be packed a bit on the loose side. This must be carried out, painstaking though it may be, so that a char will begin to form at the very bottom of the bowl. Too often a novice (or even a confirmed) pipeman will only smoke about half the bowl, either because he is unable to keep it lit longer to finish the bowl or because he finds this bottom tobacco somewhat distasteful. What happens? Only the upper half of the bowl is charred, the rest being raw and unseasoned by the flavorful tobacco. It is a perplexing circumstance and can lead to a crack or a burn-out—two calamitous climaxes. So . . . by smoking only a quarter of a bowl for a while we eliminate this danger, secure in our knowledge that we shall never encounter this malaise in the future when, as invariably happens, the pipe is not just a device for smoking but an old and trusty companion.

Subsequently, the level of filling should be gradually elevated. After the initial five (5) smokes, smoke ten (10) half bowlfuls. Then ten (10) three-quarter filled bowls, and finally, but only after the prescribed twenty-five (25) incomplete, you will have truly earned the privilege of a full pipe. If these measures seem a trifle drastic, remember this: Be not too hasty at first and your compensation will be abundant; a pipe gives pleasure not for a mere moment, but for a lifetime.

On Filling the Pipe

How often have you seen some fellow crudely thrust this pipe into the dark depths of his tobacco pouch, unthinkingly shovel, cram, and ram tortured leaves into the bowl, and then yank it out most brutally only to suppose he has filled his pipe? Well, he may have a full pipe, but he has certainly not filled his pipe. Filling the pipe, it should be noted, is in no mien or manner related to stuffing a turkey: rather, it is an artful chore that must be cultivated, a necessary task that precedes the Ceremony of the Match.

But before considering the actual filling, it is first to make absolutely certain that no shreds of unburned tobacco linger in the bowl or stem. Check by peering down into the bowl and by blowing briskly down the stem. Any shreds that cannot be blown away must be removed by means of either a pipe cleaner or a metal pick. Old scraps are grossly unpleasant as they can ruin the fragrance and taste of the new tobacco.

Once the pipe has been cleared, the filling can begin. The priority here to *evenness*; this, coupled with proper lighting technique, is the key to what is very often the prime deterrence for prospective pipe smokers—the pipe refuses to stay lit. An evenly packed pipe is the best method for preventing this. In filling, the fundamental rule is this: Pack your pipe by pinches, a pinch approximately equaling one loosely packed thimbleful of tobacco. Start by placing a pinch at the bottom of the bowl, setting it in place tenderly. The tobacco used for this pinch should be composed of the longest and/or largest shreds; this to avert accidental inhalation of tobacco "dust," the almost powdery tobacco that usually comes with most tins.

In filling the pipe pinch by pinch, each successive pinch should be set in place a bit more firmly than its predecessor. The filling should be periodically checked by drawing through the pipe: If there is virtually no resistance, then you should begin to pack tighter; if on the other hand the draw is insufferably arduous, like sucking a thick malted through a straw, then there is only one solution—empty the pipe and begin again. A too loose pipe can be remedied, but a too tight one cannot. Once the pinches begin to approach the brim of the bowl, the fatty underside of the thumb is the only rammer to be used. This is to ensure an even lighting surface. Packed in this prudent manner, it should take as many as five or six pinches before the job is done; the tobacco should feel somewhat springy to the touch, resilient to the thumb's gentle prodding.

It must be mentioned here that the dangers of uneven packing are manifold. First of all, an unevenly packed pipe cannot stay lit as it should. The fire cannot burn evenly and smoothly when it has to jump from one side of the pipe to the other to find a hospitable place to burn. Looser tobacco burns faster than the more tightly packed, and if there is loosely packed tobacco on one side primarily, then just one side of the pipe will burn. Remember, a well-filled pipe does not need cajoling match after match after match.

Perhaps more important, the unevenly filled pipe can only produce an unevenly charred pipe. A lopsided char, of course, is an ailment of grave concern, responsible for a battery of evils; inability to stay lit, burnout potential, and even foulness due to the excessive collection of tobacco juices are just a few. Thus, in filling your pipe, learn to set the pinches carefully and exactly, increase the pressure slightly with each pinch—finishing with the thumb only—and, above all, exercise patience: It is an art all pipe smokers should master.

On lighting the pipe

The procedure for lighting the pipe, and for sustaining it, involves four fundamental steps. First, the tobacco having been leveled by the thumb, strike a wooden match (paper matches disintegrate too quickly) and hold it over the bowl so that when you draw in, the flame dips readily into the tobacco. Our goal here is to ignite the entire surface with one match; therefore, the match should travel in a circle around the inside perimeter of the bowl. In turn, this should cause the outer area to catch fire, setting a blaze around the central core. Once the outside is caught, then the core should speedily ignite in like fashion and, in one fell swoop, the tobacco shall be lit.

Immediately, you will notice that the uppermost layer of the tobacco has begun to writhe and curl in a most fanciful way. It is at this point that step number two begins. For this operation a metal tamper is invaluable; this tool can be purchased at all pipe shops. So, with a tender touch tamp down the upstart shreds of tobacco until the surface has been restored to its former levelness. Due to the burning that has occurred up to now, the surface will appear an ashy gray, and, due to the tamping, it may be dead, that is unlit. The evenness restored, step three is in order.

It is this step that might be called the true lighting, for with this ignition the blaze spreads evenly over the entire surface and, in so doing, penetrates into the body of tobacco beneath that patiently awaits its fiery executioner. The lighting should be carried out as before, the match circling the core, dipping its flame into the tobacco leaf. Once caught, the pipe should be smoked tenderly, never stoking it up like a furnace, but drawing steadily, leisurely, and with deliberate placidity.

Once approximately three-quarters of the tobacco has been consumed, the pipe very often dies. At this point, many smokers consider the pipe finished, empty it out, and retire it to the rack. However, the remnant tobacco, sometimes called the "dottle," is an especially invigorating part of the pipeful. More moist, more nicotine-charged, and more difficult to smoke, it is considered by some to be a delicacy, the previous three-quarters being just an obligatory chore. In truth, the dottle does possess a uniquely innervating *esprit* that must be experienced by all pipe enthusiasts. To smoke this dottle, and so advance to the fourth step, first carefully evict all ashes from the bowl, trying not to disturb the dottle itself. Then tamp it down just a bit and light as before. In this manner the tobacco can be finished to the last shred, and with only three matches.

Another and altogether different lighting

technique, one that has been in use for more than a few centuries, is to place a burning ember of wood atop the tobacco. Among pipe connoisseurs, this method ranks as the *ne plus ultra*, affording a luxurious aroma and taste as well as effectively doing the job. To do so, use an ember of some odoriferous wood, such as pine or spruce, and place it on the tobacco. The ember, being denser than the ash, will naturally descend according to the level of the unconsumed tobacco, sinking, if you wish, to the very bottom, ever fanning the fires and imparting a perfume that compliments tobacco rarely.

On cleaning the pipe

I have heard barbarians equate the alluring aroma of the pipe with the stink of a cheap cigar. It is truly a pity not only because the pipe is to a cheap cigar as champagne is to Kool-Aid but because the whole smelly situation is entirely avoidable. Let us beware: There is no reason on earth why a pipe should smell so wicked other than the systematic neglect of its owner to keep it clean. A dirty pipe smells horrid, it is true, but a clean pipe may be likened to a spring bouquet. The pipe, as we have seen, is no casual toy for an idle moment: It is and involves a discipline—one that rewards its disciples in pleasure unbounded. But to partake of the pleasure, we must tend to the chores, one of which is cleanliness.

Of all the pipe's many accessories, not a one is so essential as the simple pipe cleaner. No pouches, racks, humidors, or tools can usurp its supreme position. Once the pipe has been smoked to your satisfaction, there is a simple regimen that should be followed religiously. First, loosen the ash with a pick and knock it free of the bowl; then, with a full breath, blow down the stem and scatter the dusty ash that remains. Now, run a fresh pipe cleaner through the stem and down into the shank and, with a brisk back and forth action, let the pipe cleaner do its work. To withdraw the soiled pipe cleaner, push it deeper still until it emerges inside the bowl and, with a quick tug, pull it up through. Pulling the cleaner back through the stem, as so many persist in doing, only defeats its purpose. This easy chore will prevent the build-up of juices in the stem and shank.

After every ten smokes or so a major clean-up is in order. These six steps are particularly vital to the pipe's health; they keep it young, sensitive to the tobacco, alive and kicking, so to speak.

1. *Break the pipe*; that is, separate the ebonite stem from the briar shank. In doing this, never pull the stem directly off—this is the best way to break it! Rather, *twist* the stem out gently but firmly. Besides ensuring against breakage, twisting maintains a tighter fit at this crucial junction.

2. *Clean the stem* by running a fresh pipe cleaner through it. If you like, a little liquid pipe cleaner or isopropyl alcohol can be used to moisten the tip of the cleaner. Then, run a dry pipe cleaner through the stem, dry the outside of any excess liquid cleaner, and set the stem to one side.

3. *Clean the tenon hole* with a pick and a fresh pipe cleaner. A very overlooked part of the pipe, this is where unsavory residue can build up for years undetected. If left unchecked, it will cause a soggy shank and hence a foul undertaste to the smoke.

4. *Clean the shank* by folding a pipe cleaner over double and running it through several times. The smallest touch of isopropyl alcohol can be applied to the pipe cleaner before inserting it.

5. *Clean the bowl* by twisting a rag or paper towel into an appropriate shape and "screw" it deeper and deeper into the bowl. A little isopropyl alcohol may be used.

6. *Dry the pipe* thoroughly by leaving it where fresh air can flow in and around it. (A windowsill is perfect.) Leave it be for a full twelve hours and then re-join the stem and the shank.

Under the heading of cleaning falls the vital operation of reaming. To keep a pipe in perfect repair, it should be reamed at least once a year, twice if it has been heavily smoked. Reaming is nothing more than cutting away enough of the char so that its thickness measures no more than a sixteenth of an inch. It is important not to attempt reaming with an object not specifically designed for that purpose. A kitchen knife, knitting needle, or chisel cannot do the job: chips and massive unevenness will be the least damage, ruining a char that took a year to build up, perhaps longer. A tool especially for reaming, called, appropriately enough, a reamer, can be purchased at most pipe shops. Generally, reamers are adjustable and fit all pipes.

The Perfect Mistress

The bed was soon made ready; and the visitor, declining all refreshment but a cup of tea, retired. Then Dot—quite well again, she said, quite well again—arranged the great chair in the chimney corner for her husband; filled his pipe and gave it to him; and took her usual little stool beside him on the hearth. . . . She was, out and out, the best filler of a pipe I should say, in the four quarters of the globe. To see her put that chubby little finger in the bowl, and then blow down the pipe to clear the tube; and when she had done so, affect to think that there was really something in the tube, and blow a dozen times, and hold it to her eye like a telescope, with a most provoking twist on her capital little face, as she looked down it; was quite a brilliant thing. As to the tobacco, she was perfect mistress of the subject; and her lighting of the pipe, with a wisp of paper, when the Carrier had it in his mouth—going so very near his nose, and yet not scorching it—was Art, and high Art, Sir.
—Charles Dickens
The Cricket on the Hearth

Porcelain

The porcelain pipe, long a favorite if not a trademark of the Alpine peoples, is singular in its qualities. Superficially, the pipe is striking: The flexible curved bit bends to meet the long and slender cherrywood stem,

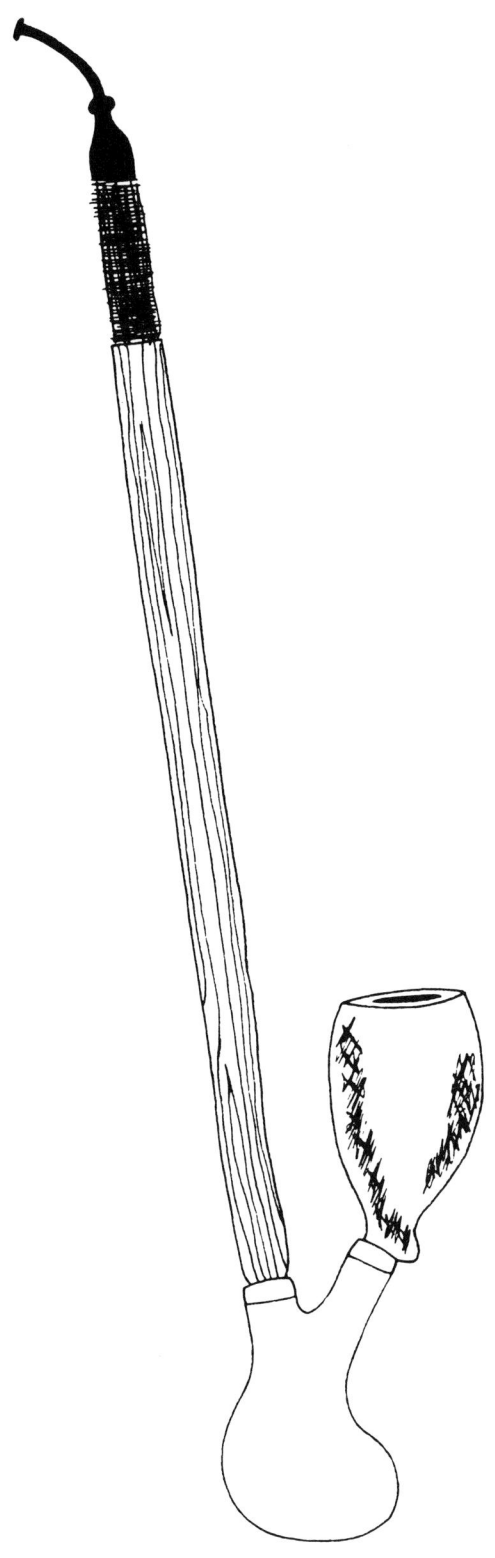

in itself a thing of lithesome coupling that fairly flows to its double-bowled terminus; and therein especially lies the pipe's comeliness. The upper bowl, that which contains the tobacco, and the bottom bowl, that which collects the unsavory juices, are both made of porcelain. Like fine china, porcelain admits to beauteous decoration. Colored glazes can be applied before firing and the result, if the painter is an artist, can be remarkably stunning. Generally, the upper bowl is the one that is so attended to, scenes of courtly love, pastoral and even politics gracing the shapely and capacious bowl. The bottom bowl is usually pure lily white, rounded or crescent-shaped and a compliment to both stem and upper bowl. And that is the story exteriorly.

But the prudent piper should not consider just Beauty; indeed, if Beauty is not tempered with Truth, then the pipe is a sorry failure. In this instance, however, it is not so much the pipe's Truth that must be looked after but the smoker's. The porcelain is a pipe of great sensitivity: if not treated with the utmost care, the pipe will invariably and irretrievably dilapidate. For one thing, porcelain is a terribly delicate stuff for pipes, and upon lighting the tobacco inside the bowl, it is likely to crack if not smoked very moderately. The heat that is generated from the inside is conducted quite efficiently to the exterior surface; consequently, a spider's web of cracks may be the result of a pipe smoked too hastily or packed too tightly. If, to carry the potential damage to its furthest demise, the cracks become too pronounced, there is even the likelihood that oily substances that are the result of combustion will leak right through the walls of the bowl—a miserable consequence. For these reasons, it is advisable to (1) pack a porcelain pipe loosely and (2) smoke it slowly. After some time, the porcelain begins to color and, in so doing, becomes more inured. Once this coloring has taken place, there is every chance that the pipe will enjoy many years of good health and render fine service to its owner.

Another item to be wary of is the condition of the bottom bowl. This, sometimes referred to as the "chamber pot," is where the tobacco juices are collected and, if left undisturbed, here they sit, exuding nasty odors and tastes. Therefore, though this is a sane idea in theory, it can be a disastrous one in practice if the smoker does not religiously attend to its cleanliness. The theory behind this innovation is, of course, to eliminate the chance of juices trickling up through the stem and thereby reaching the mouth, and this it does very effectively. This benefit, however, is nullified if the bowl is not kept scrubbed.

The pipe made of porcelain, then, makes no small demands on its smoker. Great patience must be exercised in its seasoning, and constant care is required to maintain it. Hard work, it has been said, never goes unrewarded. Genius may be neglected but hard work never. True to this adage, the porcelain does remunerate its attentive owner: if, after the pipe has been brought to color without undue crackage and the "chamber pot" is cleaned regularly, the smoker can expect a flavorful, mellow smoke, dry and cool from its long journey up the stem. And it is a predictable pipe, a consistently good puffer, and one that pleases the eye as well as the palate.

Corncob

The corncob pipe, or as it is lovingly called "the barnyard briar," had a rather unpropitious beginning in the sleepy river town of Washington, Missouri. According to local legend, a Dutch immigrant farmer by the name of John Schranke had been whittling corncobs into pipes for a number of years. He never sold any, probably because he didn't think anyone would be interested in such a crude pipe, just made and smoked them on his farm. Possibly no one would ever have heard of the corncob pipe if one day he hadn't decided to hitch his horse to a buckboard and ride into town to visit his friend, Henry Tibbe. Tibbe, who operated a woodworking shop, was turning a spindle on his lathe just as Schranke arrived. Well, farmer that he was, Schranke had never heard of a lathe before, much less seen one in action, but as soon as he did, the idea immediately flashed upon him. In another moment, he had produced a corncob from his coat pocket, handed it to Tibbe, and told him what to do with it. It wasn't long before Schranke was lighting up the first machine-made corncob pipe, praising Tibbe's handicraft as well as the delicious taste and smell of the pipe. Old Tibbe had never seen anything quite like it, but darned if he didn't think it was all right. In another hour he had turned out several such pipes, and he hung them in his window with a "for sale" sign. Another hour and they had all been sold, all to passers-by who were enthralled by these remarkable things. And thus it was, a little more than a hundred years ago, that the corncob pipe industry got its start.

In 1970 the president of the largest corncob pipe industry in the world, still using

Tibbe's old workshop for its headquarters, estimated that about ten million corncob pipes would be sold that year.

There are many things to be said for the humble corncob, but nothing pays it greater tribute than this: Since 1872 the corncob has acquired a loyal if not rambunctious following that stretches from Sidney to Sweden. Listed in its roles included such famous corncob men as the poet Carl Sandburg, the generals Pershing and MacArthur, and President Hoover. That all these dignitaries are now dead can in no way be attributed to their infatuation with the corncob.

Unique in its qualities, the corncob possesses a profound appeal for the novice. Unlike other pipes, it requires very little, if any at all, breaking in. Caution may be the rule for other pipes, but carefree abandon is characteristic of the corncob. "Cram her full clar to th' brim with nachral leaf," as the poet said, on your very first smoke. It will give surprising satisfaction, never hot and always refreshingly piquant, faintly reminiscent of Pilgrim Thanksgiving and altogether enjoyable.

One of the corncob's most frequently touted qualities is its uncanny ability to absorb moisture; it fairly sponges up the juices of the tobacco. For a very great number of smokers this is the pipe's highlight and attraction. There is however one major impediment that prevents the cob from taking its place beside the meerschaum, for, unlike that burnished queen, the corncob pipe will eventually reach its level of saturation, and if the smoker is too impatient, the pipe will fall to soggy ruin. Impatient, I say, because this situation can be avoided. To avert this unfortunate situation, the pipe must be allowed to dry out thoroughly between each and every smoke, no exceptions. Once the supersaturation process begins, there is no turning back, and if left to run its odious course, the pipe would "stink like hell," as one of the industry's representatives put it.

But the corncob is not, like the briar, a thing eternal. Indeed, like an athlete, it steadily matures, reaches its peak, and then, sometimes rather suddenly, slides downhill. Trust a corncob to last a good six months; after that watch for signs of deterioration: bitter taste or unsavory odor or even physical decay if it's had a hard life. Though I have no proof, I have heard of corncobs lasting up to two years; with loving care, I suppose this, too, is possible.

How To Make A Corncob Pipe

To make a corncob pipe it is essential to use the largest ear of corn you can get. One variety, called hog corn because it is fed to livestock, is very good, having a nice woody cob and one that is thick. Actually, any ear of corn that has a large cob will be all right. When you get the corn home, take a kitchen knife and scrape off the kernels. These should be cooked in a little salted water, buttered and eaten, for the next step is a long one, and you may work up an appetite. Turn your oven on to around one hundred and fifty degrees, put the cob in, and wait around five hours. This dries it out to a point where it can be worked.

After the five hours has elapsed, take the cob out of the oven and cut a two-inch section from its middle, this being the thickest portion. This, of course, is the bowl, and like all bowls it must have a tobacco hole. To

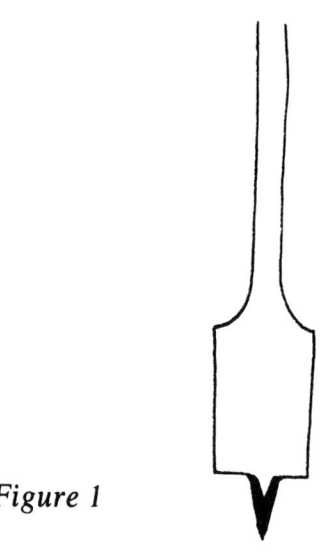

Figure 1

bore this hole it is best to use a modified wood-boring bit such as is illustrated in Figure 1. Use a flat file to cut down the spur. Generally speaking, a half-inch hole is sufficient, but for larger cobs a three-quarter-inch hole may be desirable. When drilling, leave about a half inch or even a bit more at the bottom and at least three-eighths of an inch for the walls of the bowl. (See Figure 2.) Then, return the section to the oven (same temperature) for about an hour and a half, or until the inside has thoroughly dried.

When the bowl is thus dried, take a flat file (not too coarse) and file down the cob until it is fairly smooth. Don't file it roughly, just enough to remove the unevenness.

For the stem, we have several choices. (See Figure 3.) A slim length of bamboo makes an attractive and tasty stem. Or, if you can't get any bamboo, you can whittle one from a straight twig. Get a twig about a half inch round (you can leave the bark on if you like or else strip it and polish the wood) and drill an eighth-inch hole it its center. Carve it down at one end so that it will fit into the side of the bowl and shape the other end for a mouthpiece. (See Figure 3, middle.) If you really want to get professional, you can always put on an ebonite stem, instructions for which are given in the section on briar pipe making. Drill a hole in the side of the bowl commensurate with the diameter of the stem, and stick her in. (See Figure 4.) You can always whittle the stem down some more if the fit is too tight, but you can't make the hole smaller: therefore,

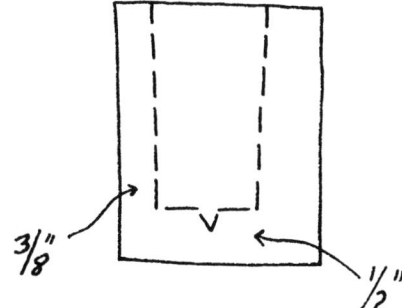

Figure 2

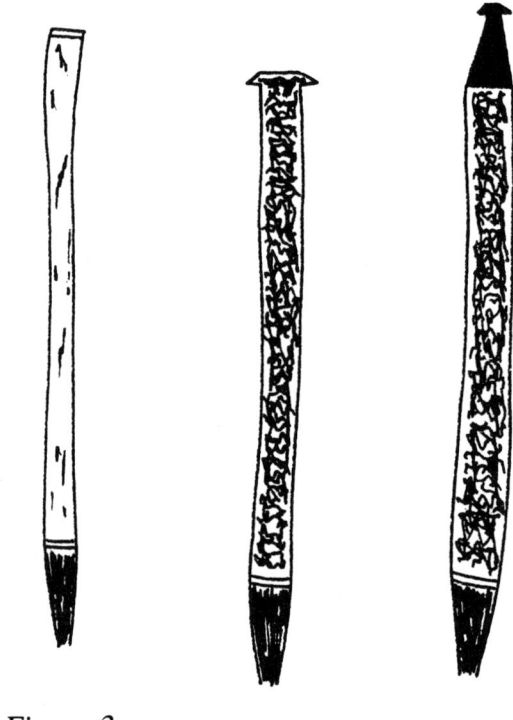

Figure 3

start with a smaller hole in the side of the bowl; if necessary, it can always be enlarged.

After you've got a good fit, take the stem out as there's some more work to be done on the bowl. To make the bowl smooth uniformly, fill all the little spaces with some plaster of Paris. Don't lay it on too heavily, just enough to round it out. Also, be sure to let it dry completely before proceeding. Then, with some medium-grade sandpaper, sand down the plaster until it has no rough edges. It will still be a little uneven but not so bad as before. Then use a fine sandpaper to smooth it out. When the bowl is pretty well sanded, take some orange-colored varnish and brush it lightly on the exterior surfaces of the bowl. Again, let dry thoroughly.

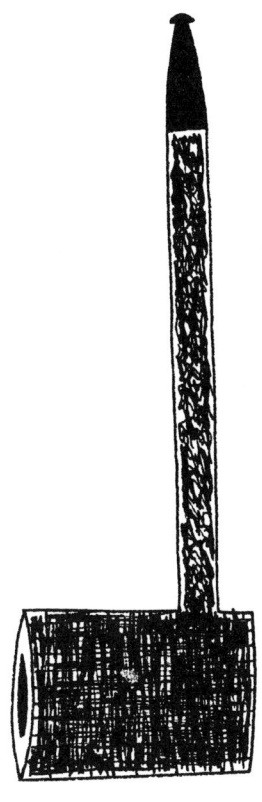

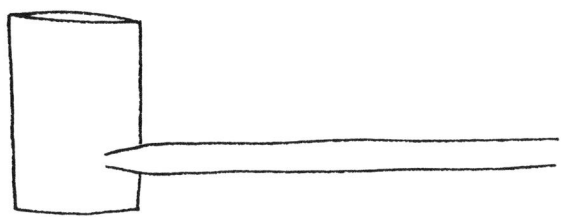

Figure 4

To insert the stem for the final time, it's a good idea to set it in with some waterproof glue. Don't let any of the glue seep into the bowl; rather, it should be a light coat on the part of the stem that sits inside the wall of the bowl and a little heavier application to the outside junction of bowl and stem. Let the glue set overnight. The pipe will be ready for its first smoking the following morning, which, I might add, is a splendid time of day for the corncob.

NINE CURIOUS CONTEMPORARIES

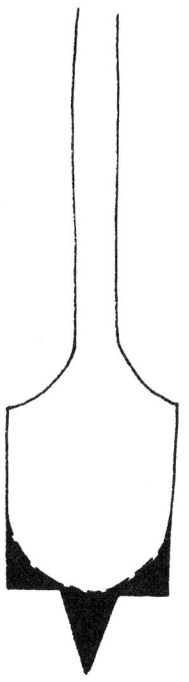

The modified three-quarter inch wood-boring bit, illustrated above, is made by filing off the edges. It is possible, too, to cut off the spurs initially with a hacksaw and then file them down to the required shape. When using this bit, it is a good idea to first drill the hole with a quarter-inch twist drill: this serves to clear a pathway for the cumbersome wood-boring bit and in so doing prevents its "running" over the surface of the wood, thus assuring an accurate hole.

This bit is especially helpful for drilling the hole in the bowl, producing a tapered but rounded interior.

A Multiple-passage Tree Pipe

This is an easy-to-make pipe that's always handy to have around. Good for just about any kind of smoking, it's capable of handling up to six smokers at once.

To make it, get a section of tree that's about three to five inches across and about two or three inches deep. Leave the bark intact.

For this particular pipe it really isn't necessary to use a hardwood; in fact, some of the softer woods may be more desirable. Pine, spruce, cherry, maple, oak—these are all fine, and when they are made into pipes, they give off a pleasing aroma of the forest.

The tobacco hole should be drilled in the top of the center of the section. The modified wood-boring bit works best here. Once that hole has been bored (see illustration), the smoke holes are next. For these holes I would advise using a quarter-inch twist drill. In the illustration only two holes are shown; any possibility, however, from one to six, is feasible. These holes should, of course, be symmetrically plotted around the pipe so as not to overload one side.

For the stem, rubber or plastic tubing is the easiest and most effective here. This can be obtained at any hardware store, generally coming in long rolls of varying lengths, diameters, grades, etc. Surgical tubing, obtainable from laboratory and hospital supply houses, is also excellent. The diameter of the tubing should be also a quarter of an inch—that is, the inside diameter. Then, into the tubing, slide a short length of quarter-inch brass tubing (obtainable at the hobby shop or hardware store) and, *voila!* you're almost ready to go.

The only thing lacking is a mouthpiece, though, if you like, the tubing itself can serve. Otherwise you'll have to either carve a suitable mouthpiece out of wood or else affix an ebonite one. The illustration shows all three possibilities. (Note: instructions for carving a wooden mouthpiece can be found

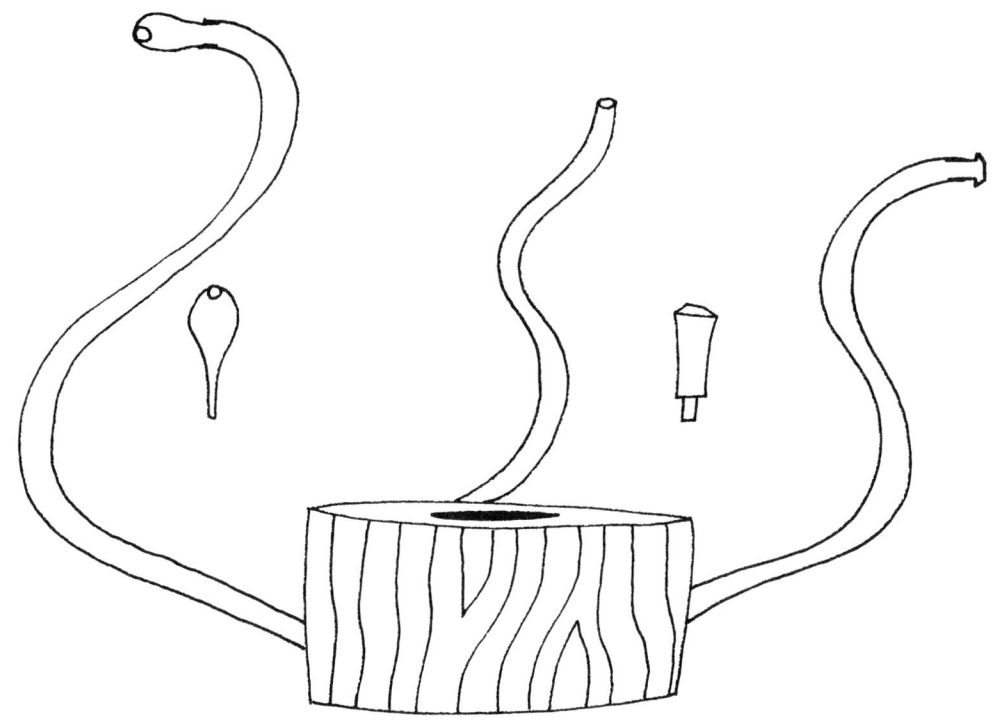

in the section of this book concerned with making a hookah; likewise, instructions for making and fitting an ebonite stem can be found in the briar-pipe-making section.)

Another thing that might come in handy is a small slip of wood that fits into the pipe and acts as a sort of plug for the stem holes that are unused. For example, if you only have three smokers and six stems, you'll want to disconnect the unused three and plug up the pipe at the three spots where the stems attach. Make several of these plugs—just little pegs a quarter of an inch in diameter and about and inch long. Keep them on hand.

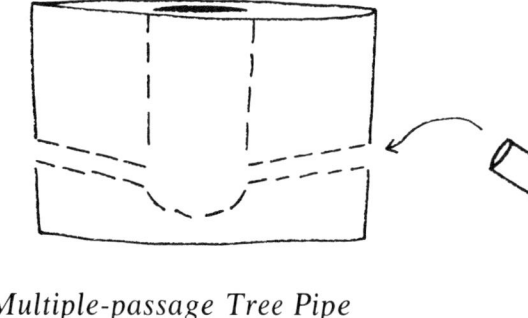

A Multiple-passage Tree Pipe

Two Dowel Pipes

Dowel pipes are perhaps the finest representative of their kind, classic *Cannabis* pipes. Good-looking and good smoking, they belong in everyone's collection.

The simpler of the two is nothing but two sections of dowel happily fitted together, one serving as the stem, the other as the bowl. First of all, go to a complete lumber yard and look over their selection of dowels. They come in lots of different sizes and designs. You should have absolutely no trouble in finding one you like.

For a fairly normal-sized pipe, get one piece about four inches long and three-quarters of an inch in diameter, and another one about two inches long and an inch and a quarter in diameter. Generally speaking, the shorter piece—that used for the bowl—should not be too curvaceous. The stem, on the other hand, can twist and convolute as much as you like.

The tobacco hole should be drilled as in the illustration, using the modified wood-boring bit or an unmodified one—here it doesn't make too much difference. The bottom of the bowl, especially if the bowl will be filled with *Cannabis*, should have a screen in it. Then, using a quarter-inch twist drill, bore a hole in the side of the bowl so as to admit the stem. Drill this hole at the angle you wish the stem to sit.

Next, take the unfinished stem and drill an eighth-inch hole through its center. You may have to drill from both ends if your bit isn't long enough—all the more reason to do this slowly. Once this smoke hole has been drilled, carve down the ends—one to fit into the bowl the other for your mouthpiece. The stem, when fitting it into the bowl, should be

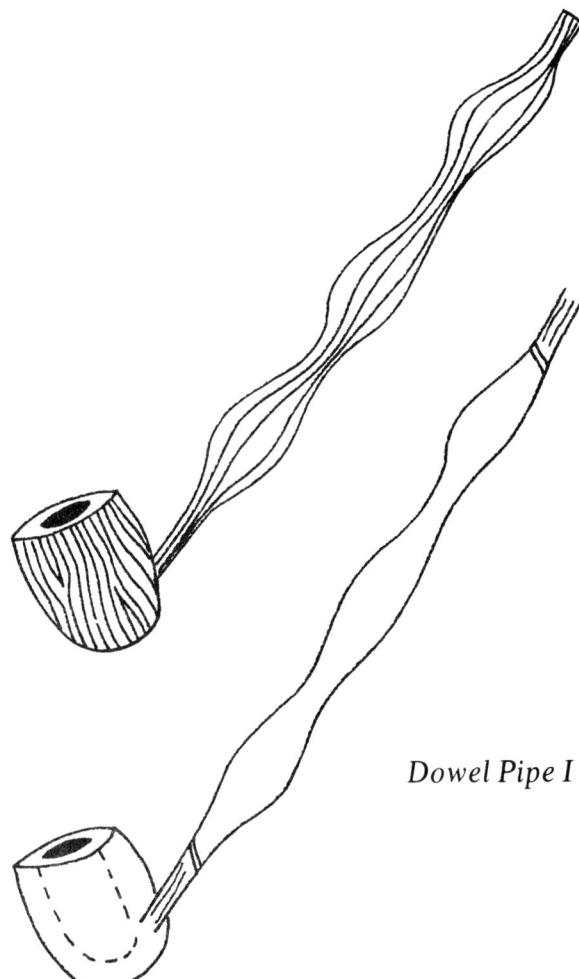

Dowel Pipe I

slipped in with a twisting action to better penetrate the opening.

With just a little more effort, the pipe can be made quite handsome. First, and before fitting the two pieces together, the bowl should be sanded down to a nice roundness. Sometimes a little filing with a flat file helps shape it. Then, stain the wood to bring out the grain. The inside of the bowl, however, should be left alone; the smoking itself will color it.

For a nice finish, wax the pipe with carnauba wax or any other high-quality furniture wax, but never varnish or shellac a wooden pipe.

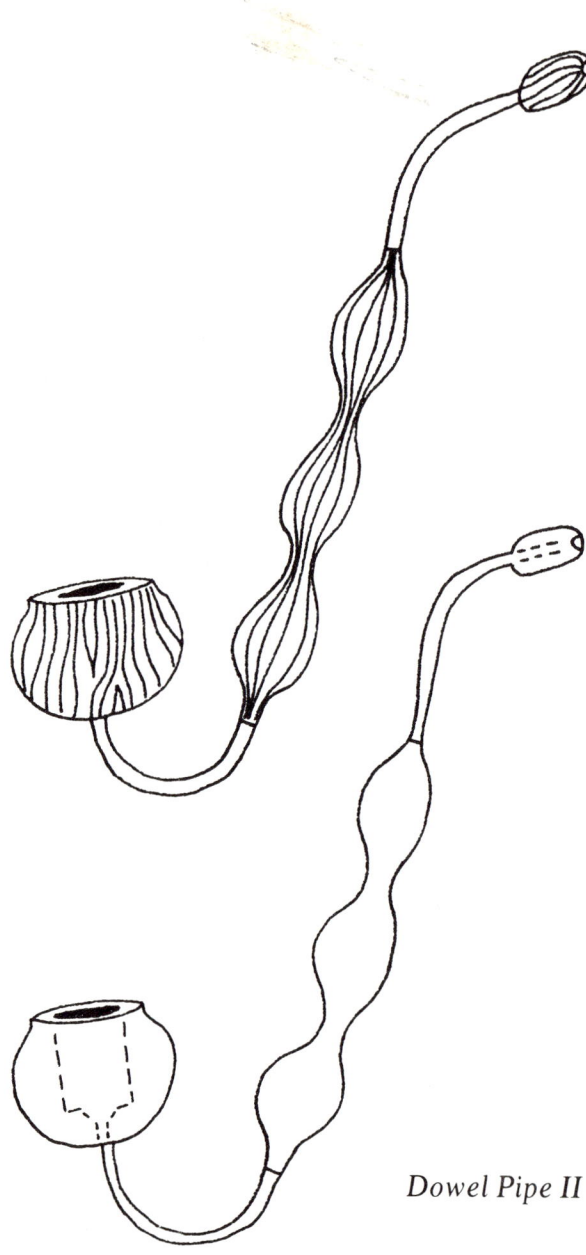

Dowel Pipe II

with the three-quarter-inch wood-boring bit (modified or unmodified) and proceed to bore right through the bowl with a quarter-inch twist drill. (See illustration.) The bowl, of course, should be shaped to its familiar roundness with a file and sandpaper.

The stem, of course, will be the brass tubing, but since this material tends to overheat, we must insulate it with another length of dowel. This piece, which should be about three inches long and about three-quarters or a half inch in diameter, should be drilled out with a quarter-inch twist drill—right through its center. Its also a good idea, artistically, to sand down the ends of this section so that when it is slipped onto the tubing it will blend in harmoniously with it. (See illustration.)

The mouthpiece for this pipe is best made from a wooden bead, obtained at the hobby shop. These beads come in a myriad of shapes, sizes, and colors, the oblong being my favorite. It will already have a hole through it, but this must be enlarged to the quarter-inch diameter—a simple job with the drill.

Now, take about a seven-inch length of quarter-inch brass tubing (quarter inch outside diameter) and put the pipe together. First, the piece of dowel for the stem is slipped onto the tubing (a dab of glue to hold it securely in place if need be); then the bowl is added (a turn of electrical tape around that end of the tubing may make it a better, tighter fit); and then the mouthpiece, also with a dab of glue, is slipped on. This completed, there is nothing left but to bend the tubing to your liking and light it up. This bending, it is good to know, should not be done abruptly; instead, bend it over a rounded surface—like a juice glass—to ensure an even sweep.

Another type of dowel pipe, and one that employs brass tubing in its design, is somewhat more elegant; curved, it is more Holmesian than the other.

To make this pipe, get a piece of dowel such as used in the other pipe for the bowl; that is, about two inches long by an inch and a quarter wide. Then, drill the tobacco hole

Finally, like the other dowel pipe, it can be sanded smooth, stained, and waxed.

A Free-form Standing Pipe

This pipe, carved from wood, makes a fine smoking pipe: its taste is never harsh, it can't overheat, and it produces such scents that can only add to the bouquet of your best blend. If possible, cut the wood for this pipe yourself—right from the tree—and season it with your own smoking mixture. You'll never find a sweeter-smoking pipe.

To make this pipe, get a piece of wood (hard or soft, but odoriferous if possible) that measures about two inches wide by two and a half inches long by one and a half inches deep. Another piece, for the stem, should be about three inches long and three-quarters of an inch in diameter.

The first thing to do is to cut it to the desired shape. (The illustration shows one that is easy to cut out and fairly good-looking.) Make sure that at least a good part of the bottom is straight—this so the pipe will be able to stand up unattended. Next, drill the tobacco hole to a depth of about an inch and a half, using the modified three-quarter-inch wood-boring bit. As the illustration shows, this is done at a little angle.

The smoke hole then should be drilled with an eighth-inch twist drill and enlarged with a quarter-inch twist drill. (See illustration.) The enlargement—to allow for the insertion of the stem—need only be for a distance of about a half inch or a bit longer.

The stem should now be bored with an eighth-inch twist drill also, its ends carved down as illustrated and all rough edges removed. The end that is to be inserted into the pipe should be about a quarter inch in diameter or a touch larger, the other end being whatever shape or size suits your

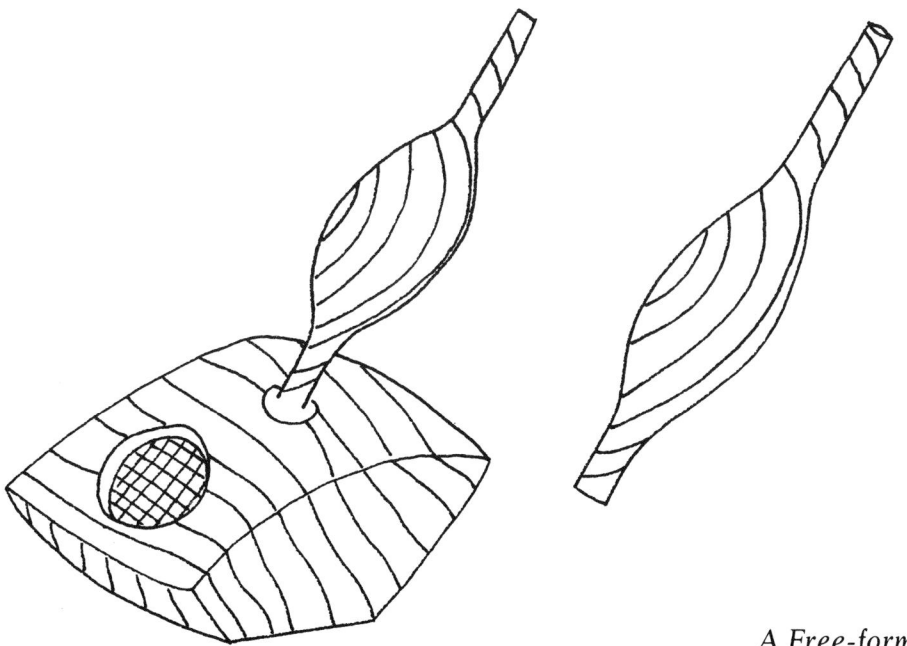

A Free-form Standing Pipe

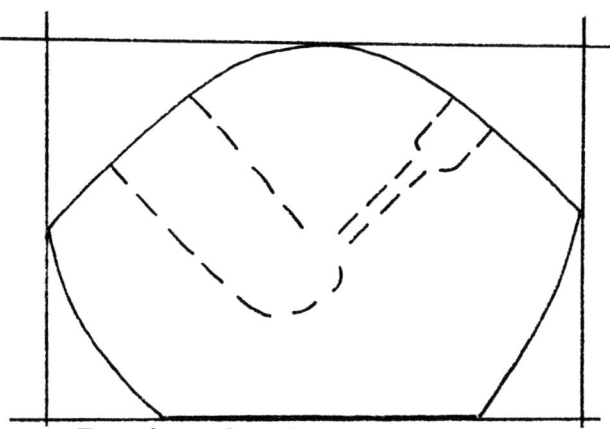
A Free-form Standing Pipe (interior view)

mouth—the plain end being perhaps the most comfortable.

To finish the pipe, sand down all edges and surfaces until they're silky smooth; stain and wax.

A Chem-lab Hookah

Anyone who has access to a chemistry lab should be able to turn up an old flat-bottom flask, a double-holed rubber stopper, and a length of glass tubing. If you don't, these things can be had very reasonably at any laboratory-supply house. The other materials—a short piece of inch and a quarter plain dowel and a length of quarter-inch brass tubing—can be purchased inexpensively at the lumber yard and the craft shop, respectively.

For the bowl assembly, use the modified wood-boring bit and go down about an inch and a half to make the tobacco hole. Then, using a quarter-inch twist drill, bore clean through the section of dowel. (See illustration.) Once the holes have been drilled, simply get out the wood rasp and file and shape the bowl as shown, sand it down, and it's finished. Into the bowl then stick a length of quarter-inch brass tubing. If necessary, wrap a few turns of electrical tape around the end of the tubing that is to be inserted into the bowl; this will make the fit tight. Also, the length of the tubing should be such that it reaches to within an inch of the bottom of the flask.

For the stem, the glass tubing should be bent at the appropriate place. (See illustration.) This can be done easily over a flame, softening the glass and then bending it slowly. Be sure to soften about an inch of the tubing to make the bend gentle rather than acute.

Once this has been done, the bowl assembly and the glass stem can be fitted into the rubber stopper, the stopper pushed into the mouth of the flask, and a screen placed at the bottom of the bowl.

A Wood Or Stone Hasheesh Pipe

This pipe, perfect for hasheesh, fits comfortably in the palm of your hand. Small enough to carry in your shirt pocket, it makes a fine compliment to the worthiest of hasheeshes.

To make it, get a piece of wood that measures three inches long by two inches wide by one inch deep. For this pipe any wood—from the softest pine to the hardest briar—is acceptable. Once you've got the wood, cut it down to the shape as indicated by the illustration, sort of a tear-drop design.

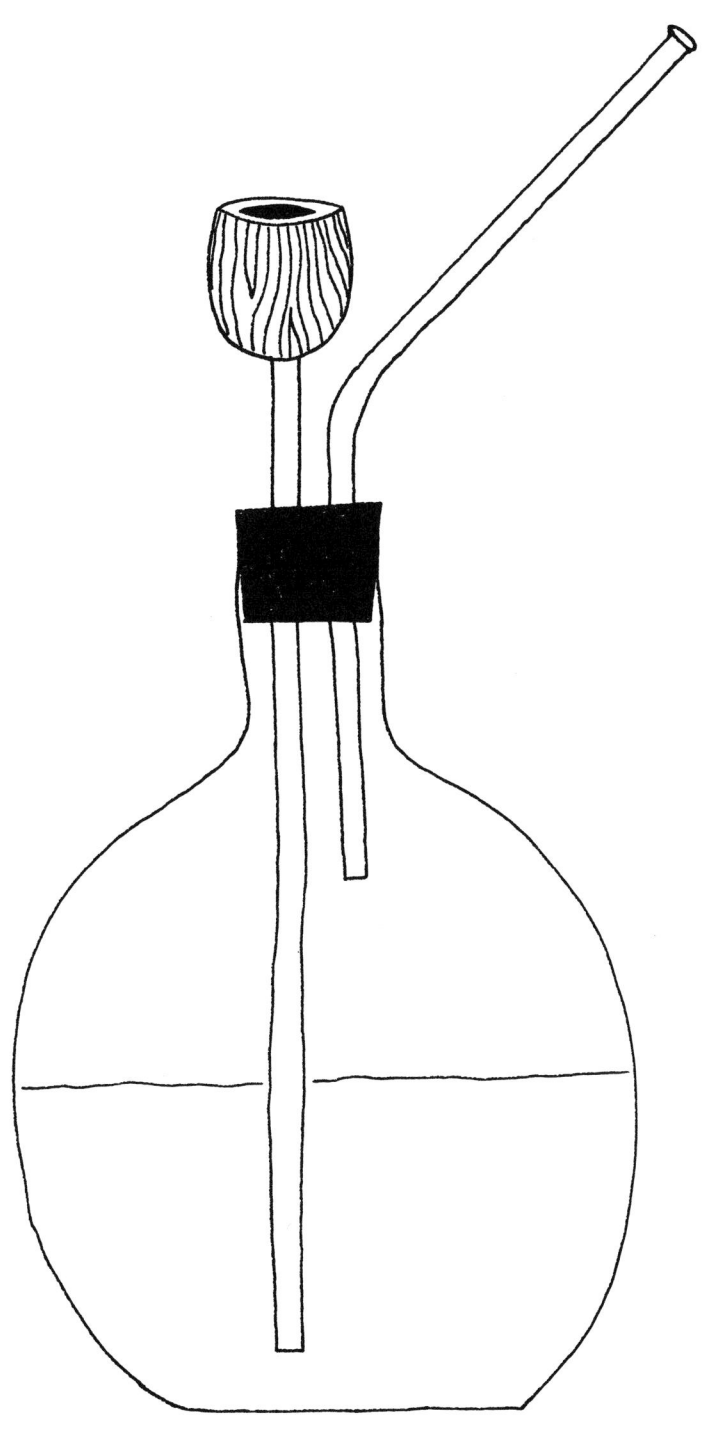

A Chem-Lab Hookah

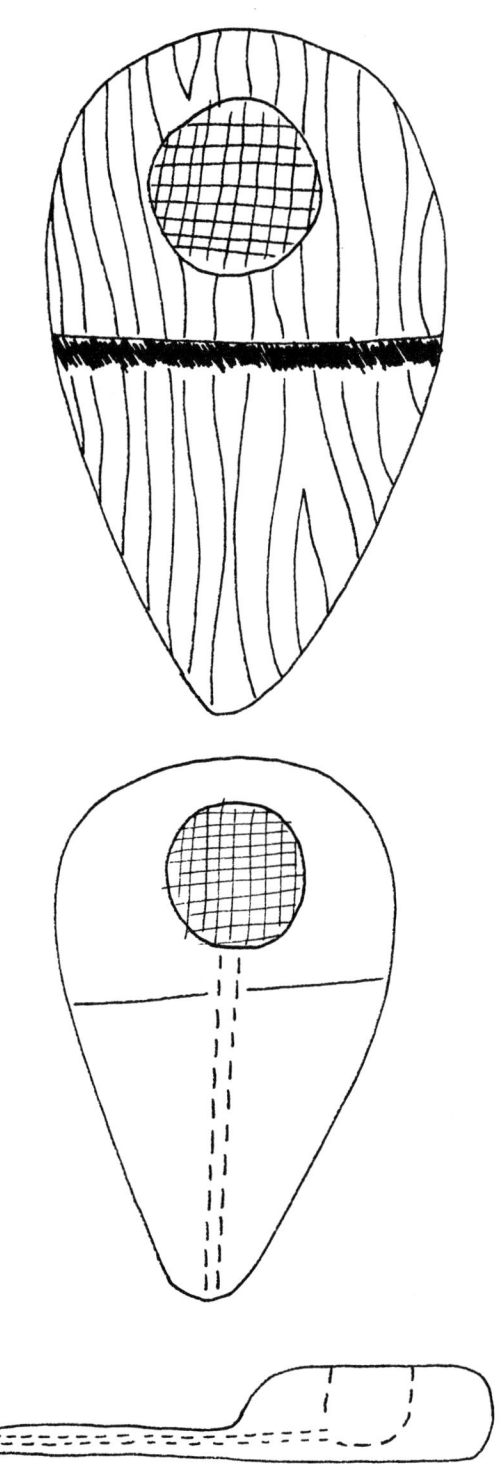

A Wood or Stone Hasheesh Pipe

The next step is to cut out the stem. About a half-inch high and extending for about two-thirds the length of the pipe, the stem can be cut with a coping saw or an ordinary wood saw. Basically, the pipe's design should now be clear and complete.

Now the raised portion of the pipe will be for the bowl. This should be bored with the three-quarter-inch modified wood-boring bit. The smoke hole, which should be drilled with a nine-sixty-fourths-inch twist drill, should be bored from the narrowest tip of the stem at a ninety-degree angle to the bowl. (See illustration.) This smoke hole drilling must be done with exacting precision; drill slowly, being sure the pipe is tightly clamped in the vise.

To finish the pipe, use a rattail file to smooth out the meeting of the bowl and stem platforms and sandpaper the entire surface, removing all the uneven spots and smoothing it all down to a curved and rounded object that feels good to hold. After sanding, the pipe should be stained and waxed and a screen dropped into the bowl.

This same pipe can also be worked from stone, a material that is particularly suited to this type of pipe. Basically, the procedure is identical except that you have to use a hacksaw, masonry bits, and metal files in place of the tools for wood. Any kind of stone can be used, but some of the softer types—such as limestone, sandstone, and soapstone—are easier to work with. The principal advantage of the stone pipe is its ability to stay cool even under heavy and prolonged smoking; with age and use, it colors beautifully.

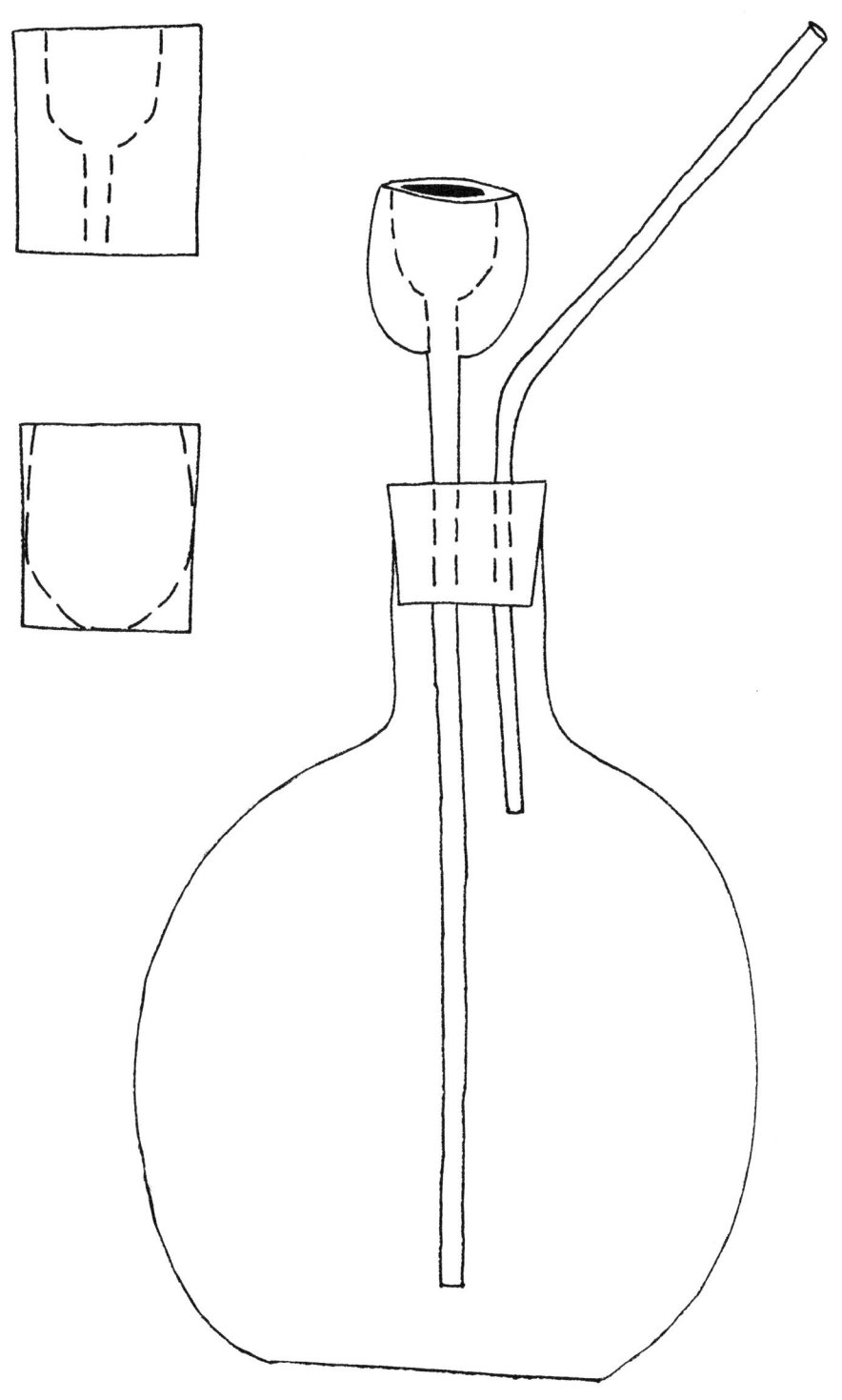

A Chem-Lab Hookah

A Water Pipe Just For Roaches

This pipe eliminates charred fingers, scorched lips, parched throat, and other maladies attributed to that potent thing—the roach. Its components—a pill bottle with a cork, a length of brass tubing, some heavy wire, an alligator clip, and a wooden bead—are simple but effective.

Get yourself a glass or plastic pill bottle and then go to the hardware store and have it fitted with a tight-fitting cork. Then, drill two holes through the cork, each three-sixteenths of an inch in diameter.

To make the stem, take a length of three-sixteenths-inch brass tubing (that you bought at the craft shop) and a wooden bead (also bought at the craft shop) and fit them together as shown in the illustration. The hole in the wooden bead will have to be enlarged to accommodate the brass tubing. Then, bend the tubing to an appropriate shape and slide it into the cork (as shown by illustration). If needed, a spot of glue both inside the hole in the cork and inside the hole in the bead will serve to hold the tubing in place.

Then, for the clip assembly, cut another length of that tubing, this to reach almost to the bottom of the bottle. It should be long enough so that at least an inch of it protrudes upwards from the cork. Onto this extension we are going to solder an alligator clip. Alligator clips are used in electronics for making connections—usually temporary—and can be purchased at stores that sell electrical supplies; some stereo-hifi stores also carry them. Now, take a short piece of wire coat hanger and bend it to a "question mark" shape. The upper part of the question mark

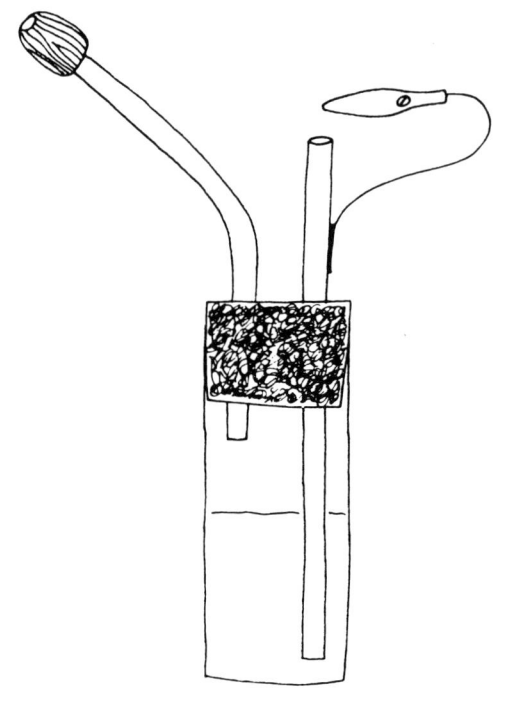

A Water Pipe Just For Roaches

slides into the alligator clip and is soldered there—just a touch of solder is necessary. In soldering, though, be sure to make it so that the clip will be sitting sideways when it is affixed to the tubing. In other words, when you are looking directly down at the pipe, you will be able to see the "jaws" of the clip. When the clip has been soldered to the wire, the wire can be soldered to the tubing. (See illustration.)

Between the clip and the opening of the tubing there should be only about an eighth of an inch or less. Solder the clip assembly onto the tubing accordingly.

Then fill the bottle half full with water, push the cork into place in the bottle's mouth, and the pipe is ready to receive its first roach.

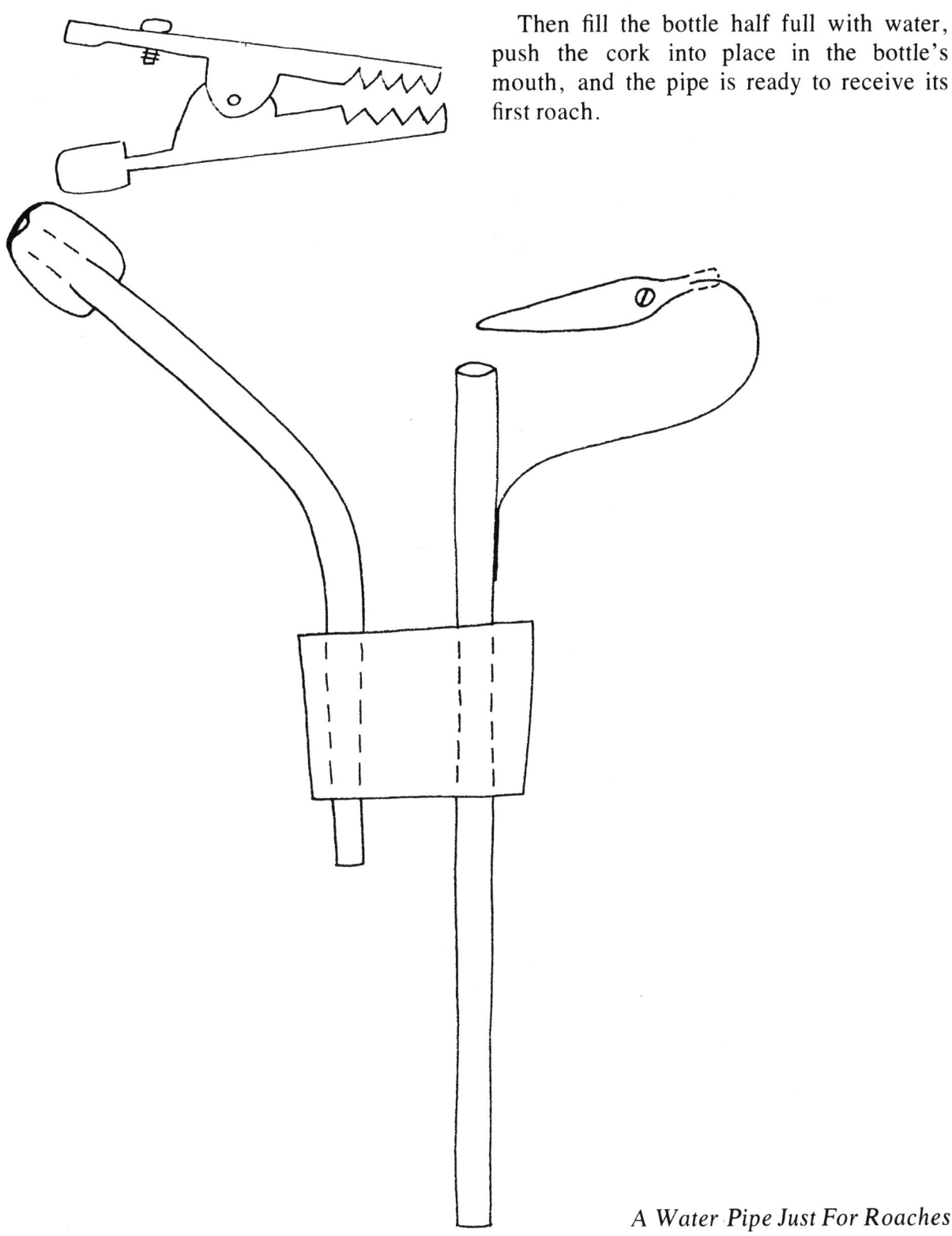

A Water Pipe Just For Roaches

Two Makeshift Pipes

If you've ever been caught in the sorry situation of having plenty to smoke but nothing to smoke it out of, here's the solution. Through the miracle of tinfoil, new avenues have been paved for the would-be smoker, and with just a little skill we can put this to work.

The first of these devices uses a cardboard tube such as is found at the end of a roll of paper towels, wax paper, toilet tissue, etc., etc. In the center of the tube, punch a hole with your finger. You can use a sharp object to get it started and then enlarge it. Then, take about a three-inch-wide strip of tinfoil and wrap it around the tube so that it covers the hole; with a finger, depress the foil into the hole you have just made, thus creating a little bowl. The foil should now be secured with a rubber band on either side.

Then, all you have to do is prick the foil bowl full of holes with a straight pin, and the pipe is made. Usual making time: one minute.

To smoke this device, hold one end of the tube to your mouth so that your lips are locked inside it. Then, with the palm of your free hand, seal off the other end. (See illustration.) The smoking mixture is then placed in the bowl, it is lit, and the makeshift pipe has saved yet another day.

Another type of makeshift, still less extravagant, requires nothing but an ordinary drinking glass, a piece of tinfoil, and a rubber band.

Over the mouth of the glass fold a square of tinfoil so that at least an inch hangs down on all sides. Then, seal it off securely with the rubber band. The bowl here is just a circle of pin pricks at one end of the foil surface, the stem but a foil-less section. Just cut away a little piece of the foil with a knife to make the stem. (See illustration.) This pipe is at its best when the glass is half filled with water; as the smoke bounces off the liquid, it is cooled.

Smoking this device is achieved by placing your lips over the end of the glass where the foil has been cut away, lighting the mixture that has been placed over the pin-pricked foil, and sucking away (as the illustration shows).

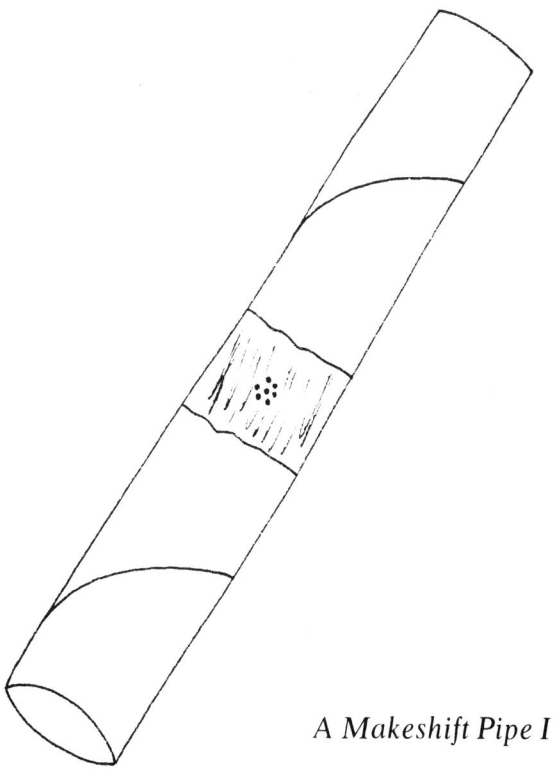

A Makeshift Pipe I

How To Smoke Makeshift Pipe I

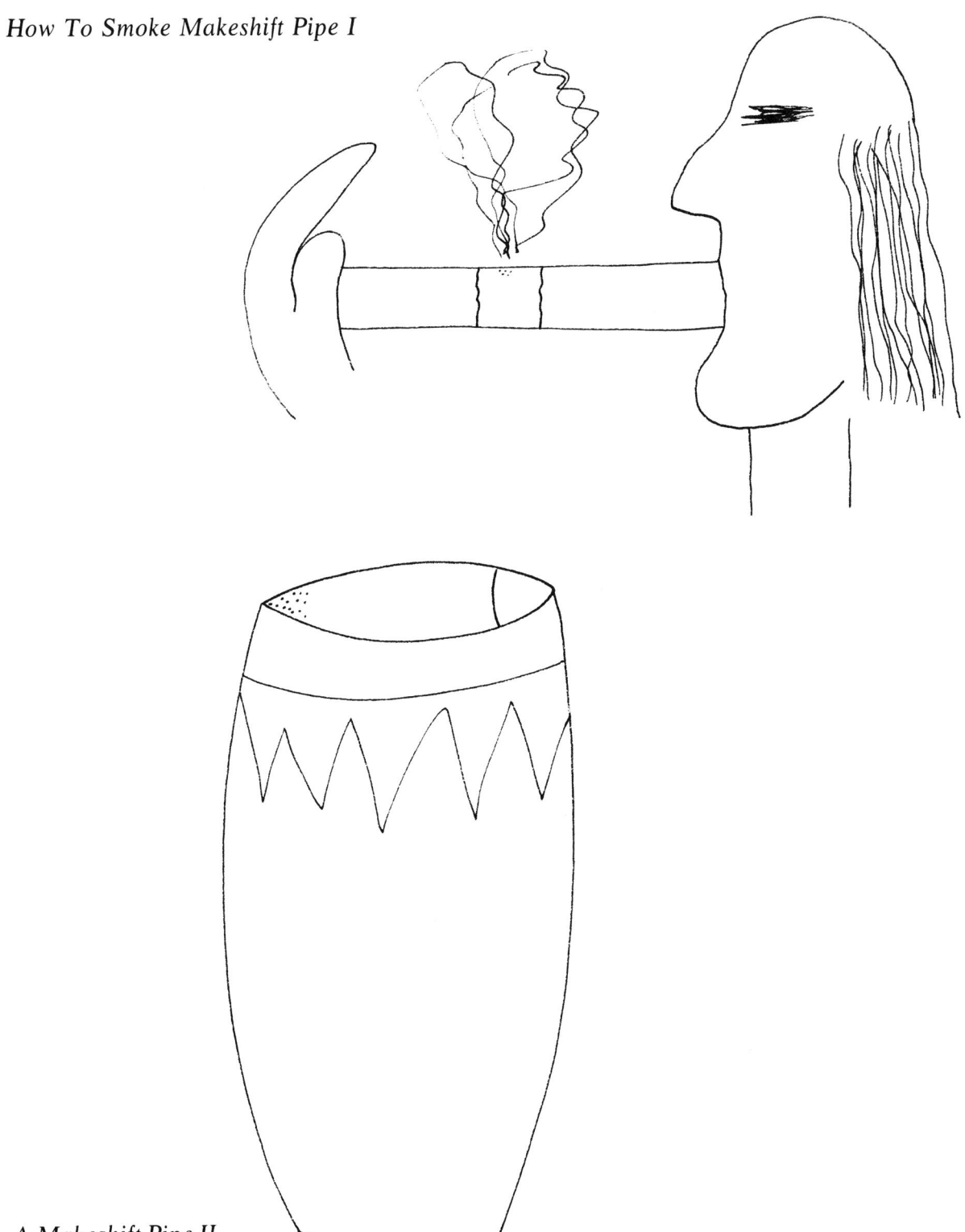

A Makeshift Pipe II

How to Smoke Makeshift Pipe II

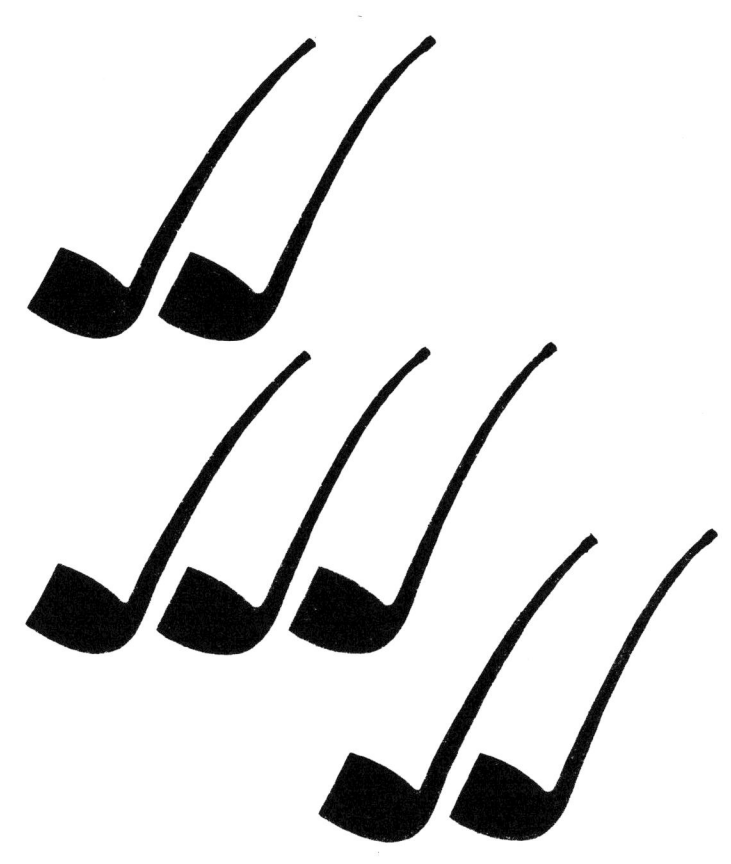

A WORD ON TOBACCO

Tobacco

If you can't send money, send tobacco.
—General George Washington,
Commander-in-Chief of the
Revolutionary Armies,
to the American people

According to the earliest and most reliable sources, the name "tobacco," as it is used today, is actually a misnomer. Before the arrival of the sailing ships from the Old World, tobacco was used to signify not the plant but the tube through which the smoke was drawn. The plant itself was known by a variety of names that changed from region to region and sometimes from tribe to tribe. Some of the more popular names for the "Indian herb" were *cohiba*, *yoli*, and *petum*. In all likelihood, when the Indian passed the pipe to the Spaniard, he said "tobacco," and it was assumed that he meant the plant being smoked rather than the pipe.

But despite the confusion, the word "tobacco" stuck, and it was by this name that all of Europe soon came to learn of this savory plant. Shortly thereafter, once the Europeans developed an insatiable appetite for the stuff, they started planting fields of it for their own consumption. This organized planting began around 1610 and has been steadily increasing to this day. In recent decades, the annual tobacco crop has been consistently in the hundreds of thousands of tons.

But in the beginning decades of tobacco cultivation, it was a cheerless though unobscure fact that there just wasn't enough tobacco to satisfy the demand. By the late 1500s the entire European continent was clamoring for more: As evidenced by the first chapter of this book, they had taken tobacco to their hearts and indeed channeled much of their attention to its acquisition and consumption. This shortage of the laudable leaf, then, led to a practice that was no doubt the subject of much controversy in its day, that of cutting the prohibitively priced tobacco with more reasonably priced ingredients. Ben Jonson, a keen observer of these conventions, has one of the characters in his play *Bartholomew Fair* speak on just this. She, a vendor of roast pig and tobacco at the fair, shouts to her tapster: "Look too't, sirrah, you were best! three pence a pipe full, I will ha' made of all my whole halfe pound of tabacco, and a quarter of a pound of *coltsfoot*, mixt with it too, to eke it out." Not the only additive to tobacco, coltsfoot, an herb of the aster family, was the one most regularly used. Other additives included rhubarb leaves, several garden herbs, and even barley meal.

But the adulteration did not end here: in an effort to sell the shoddiest leaves (which were in great abundance but nearly unbearable to smoke), the tobacco dealers often prepared these poor leaves in rather unorthodox fashion. In 1614, Doctor Barclay stated: "They sophisticate and farde [gloss over] the tobacco in sundrie sortes, with black spice, galanga, aqua vitae, Spanish wine, anise seeds, oyle of Spicke, and such like"—all this in an attempt to pass off the most impertinent tobaccos as palatable. But Ben Johnson, himself no fool, took pride in his pipe and let no charlatan corrupt his pleasure. In his *Alchemist*, he fairly adulates his tobacconist, the honest Abel Drugger, in these words which bespeak that man's noble calling:

> **He lets me have good tobacco; and he does not**
> **Sophisticate it with sack—lees or oil,**
> **Nor washes it with muscadel or grains,**
> **Nor buries it in gravel, under ground,**
> **Wrapp'd up in greasy leather, or piss'd clouts;**
> **But keeps it in fine lilly pots, that, open'd,**
> **Smell like a conserve of roses, or French beans.**
> **He has his maple block, his silver tongs,**
> **Winchester pipes, and fire of juniper.**

This practice of "sophisticating" the tobacco with all sorts of mischievous additives is one that has been propagated right up to the present. It is certainly not the infrequent advertisement that boasts its tobacco has been blasted with bourbon, chastised by cognac, candied with cherries and chocolate, or even raped by the demon Rum. And while it is true that these corrupt and debauched leaves may appeal to some, to the connoisseur they are rot. The reason for this, as Holmes said to the doctor, is elementary. Tobacco, it is crucial to our point to know this, comes in no less than forty varieties, each possessing a particular gustatory thrill. So, rather than infect the hale leaves with those very miscellaneous ingredients, the enlightened piper will select a blend of tobaccos, a mixture often consisting of up to ten different leaves.

The art of blending tobaccos, because of the endless possible combinations, is one that calls for both exactitude and a feeling for improvisation. Like a chef, the tobacconist must undergo an apprenticeship—often up to a full year. During this period, he becomes acquainted with scores of different leaves, learns to recognize their several characteristics and also their compatability with other leaves. Certain tobaccos, like certain spices, cannot be blended together. Others flatter each other to utter perfection. It is precisely these nuances that the tobacconist is trained to discern; therefore, one adept at his art should be regarded with nothing short of heartfelt admiration. Without slaughtering the essence of the tobacco, the competent tobacconist is able to produce a blend to satisfy very nearly all tastes (chocolate, root beer, etc. being the obvious exceptions). There are tobaccos that are mild, strong, dark, bright, light, heavy, sweet, bitter, nutlike, woody, pungent, bland, enervating, dour, etc., etc. Some tobaccos only have one of these characteristics; some have several, and a choice few have most. To understate the matter, it takes a skillful fellow to be able to blend ten tobaccos and come up with a palatable mixture.

Choosing a pipe tobacco has long been one of the pipe devotee's pet pastimes and, occasionally, frustrations. On the market today are countless brands and blends, each clothed in enticing tins and eulogized in flowery prose. In an attempt to clear up some of the confusion—all this tobacco to-do that can confound the indecisive customer—the following is offered.

For the pipe smoker, tobaccos have three salient characteristics: taste, fragrance, and the rate at which they burn; if the blend is to be successful, all three factors must be carefully considered. If, for instance, only fast-burning tobaccos were included in the mixture, the pipe would smoke intolerably hot. On the contrary, if only slow-burning tobaccos were blended, it would be nearly impossible to get it lit and keep it burning. Therefore, one characteristic must be tempered with another, fast-burning with slow-burning, pungent with bland, fragrant with nonodorous. Tobacconists are adept at this balancing and, generally speaking, blend tobaccos that appeal to this sense of balance that people instinctively possess. Some people, of course, like and are able to appreciate the odder blends, those containing higher percentages of the more exotic leaves. These blends are usually stronger and spicier and generally need some getting used to before their full overtures can be best appreciated.

In the business of selecting a blend, there are certain tobaccos about which it is necessary to be conversant. Then, when the list of ingredient leaves is read on the tin, it is easier to ascertain the blend's personality. Something like choosing a friend, one looks for certain characteristics that appeal to one's sensibility.

Certainly one of the better tobaccos is *Virginia*. It can either be smoked straight or blended, is relatively docile in both taste and fragrance, and burns moderately, not too fast or too slow. The Virginia leaf is one of the staples of tobacco blending. Its light fragrance and nutlike taste are very amiable in blends, providing a mellow base to which other, more titillating tobaccos can be added. One of the varieties of this tobacco, called Virginia Bright, can generally be found in blends of high-quality tobaccos. Its bright golden color, when set in contrast to the darker leaves, produces that beautiful dappled effect that is so prevalent among blended tobaccos. One good thing to be cautious about: If Virginia is smoked straight, be certain that it is cut in broad, long pieces, not minced to miniscule shreds. Virginia is not so moist a tobacco as some of the others, and there is the danger of "bite," a danger that can generally be dodged if the leaf is cut in substantial pieces.

Burley is another tobacco that can be smoked straight. It is perhaps the gentlest of all leaves and consequently the one most frequently smoked straight. Burley tobacco has precious little taste or fragrance compared to some of the other leaves, but its natural barklike savor is quite popular. In blends, burley is remarkably satisfying, being a soft backdrop for other leaves. In general, these burley leaves burn rather unhurriedly and provide a cool, languid smoke. The best-known variety is called Kentucky burley and, even smoked straight, can be most obliging.

Still another type that can be both blended and smoked straight, *cavendish* tobaccos are distinctly sweet and gay. In fact, it may very well have been the frolicsome fragrance of cavandish that first attracted you to the pipe. The rich brown leaves may appear to be on the dark and somber side, but once dispelled into smoke they become light and cheery. Cavandish burns at a sprightly pace, but because it is generally on the moist side, it is rarely hot or harsh. Honey cavandish, so named due to its semblance to the bee's best, is a noteworthy variety of this tobacco and one that represents its clan favorably in any blend.

At the other end of the spectrum, *perique* tobacco is used only as a flavoring leaf and is never smoked straight. This very pungent tobacco is cultivated only in the state of Louisiana, no other area being suitable. In blends, perique is used sparingly: one part perique to nine parts other tobacco is considered excessive. Yet when added in the correct proportion perique can contribute an indescribable flavor that is neither here nor there, but all the same very clear. Perique burns at a nice relaxed rate and steadies the burning rate for any blend it entertains. This leaf is perhaps at its best when blended with Virginia tobaccos.

Latakia tobacco is another that cannot be smoked straight but is used fairly exclusively for its robust flavor. Cured over smoldering spices and herbs, latakia has a zest that is remarkable for its ability to take a lackluster blend and give it life. A dark, damp tobacco, latakia burns very slowly, giving up its delectable oils like a miser. Latakia differs from perique in that it is spicier in an herbal sense and not so piquant as the perique. Latakia is somehow more discrete.

Under the heading of *Turkish* tobaccos are to be listed many varieties. In general, Turkish tobaccos are heavier than those cultivated in America, more aromatic, and possess a fuller taste. One of the most highly esteemed varieties is called Xanthi. Its lively aroma tends to bring out the subtleties of otherwise mediocre blends. Another variety of the Turkish tobaccos is the Macedonian. These leaves are less pronounced than the other Turkish tobaccos and can be both blended and smoked straight. Still, it is definitely rife with Turkish allusions. Every pipe smoker should get acquainted with these tobaccos since they provide an unending source of pleasurable surprise.

But the blend itself aside, all tobacco should be kept in a place that encourages the retention of all its finest qualities. Undoubtedly, a humidor tends to this chore admirably, but actually any container with a lid that can be tightly sealed is all right, too. Above all else, the leaves must be kept a trifle moist, not damp but not brittle, either. Keeping the tobacco in a sealed container helps maintain this desirable state. Tobacco that is too dried-out burns too fast; the result is that the smoke is hot and unflavorful, and this not only bites the tongue and dries up the mouth but leaves a disagreeable taste as well. If, even though the tobacco is locked in a proper container, it is still too dry, toss a slice of apple into the container with the tobacco. As the apple shrivels up, it will release moisture that the tobacco will absorb. If you have a particularly dried-out batch that cannot be revived like this, it is sometimes possible to do so by spraying the leaves with an atomizer filled with water. If, for any reason, the tobacco becomes too moist to light and keep burning, then leave the top off the container for several hours, thereby allowing some of the moisture to escape. If more drastic steps are needed, spread the tobacco out on a table in the sun for an hour. In all things, balance.

Lord Byron on Tobacco

Sublime tobacco! which, from east to west,
Cheers the Tar's labor or the Turkman's rest;
Which on the Moslem's ottoman divides
His hours, and rivals opium and his brides;
Magnificent in Stamboul, but less grand,
Though not less loved, in Wapping or the Strand;
Divine in hookahs, glorious in a pipe,
When tipp'd with amber, mellow, rich, and ripe;
Like other charmers, wooing the caress
More dazzlingly when daring in full dress;
Yet thy true lovers more admire, by far,
Thy naked beauties—Give me a cigar!

Selected Specialties and Oddities

Special Photographs
Courtesy of
The Smithsonian Institution
Washington, D.C.

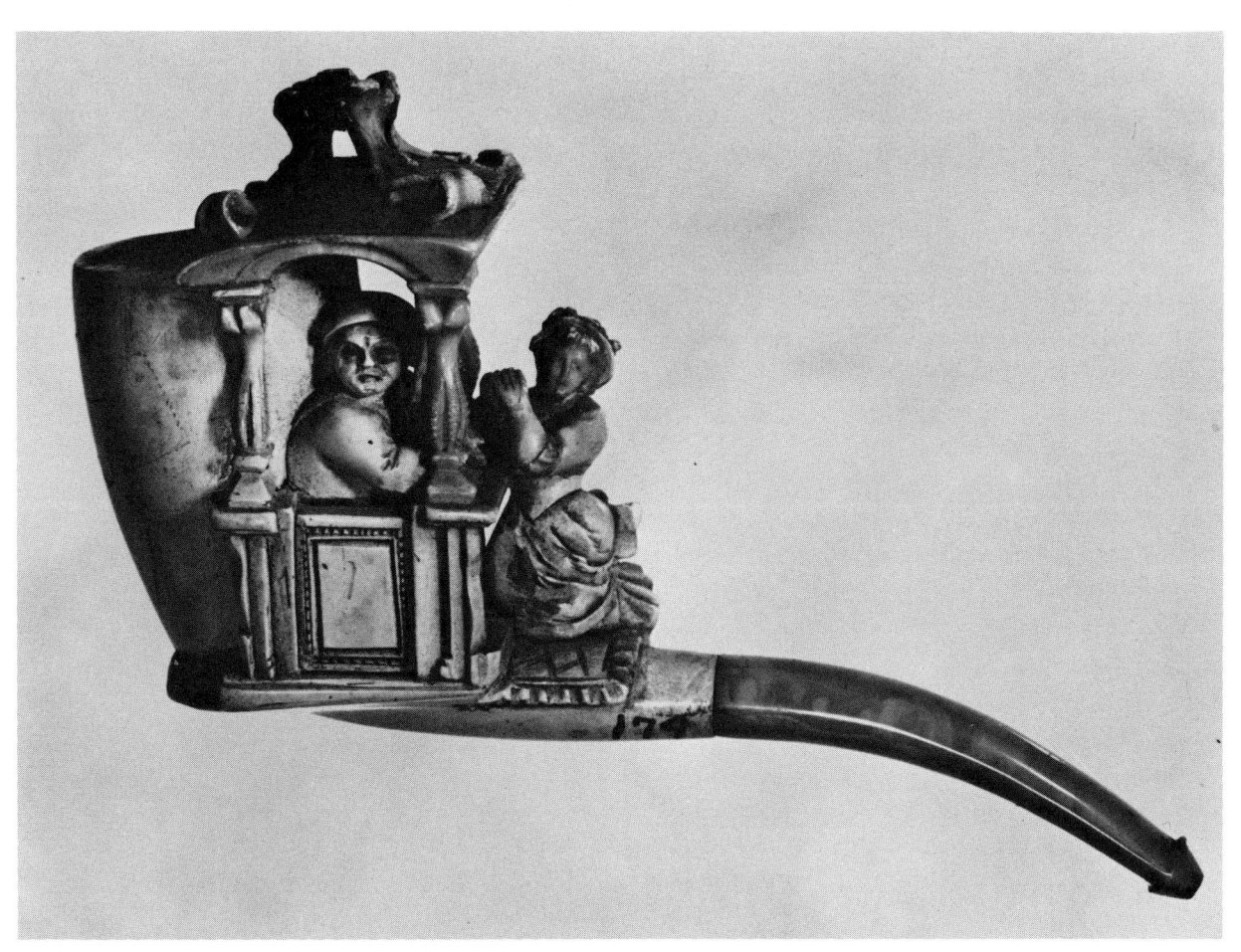

1—Meerschaum pipe with curved amber bit

2—Pipe with wooden bowl, blown glass well and turned reed-like stem; probably Italian

3—Carved wooden pipe; French

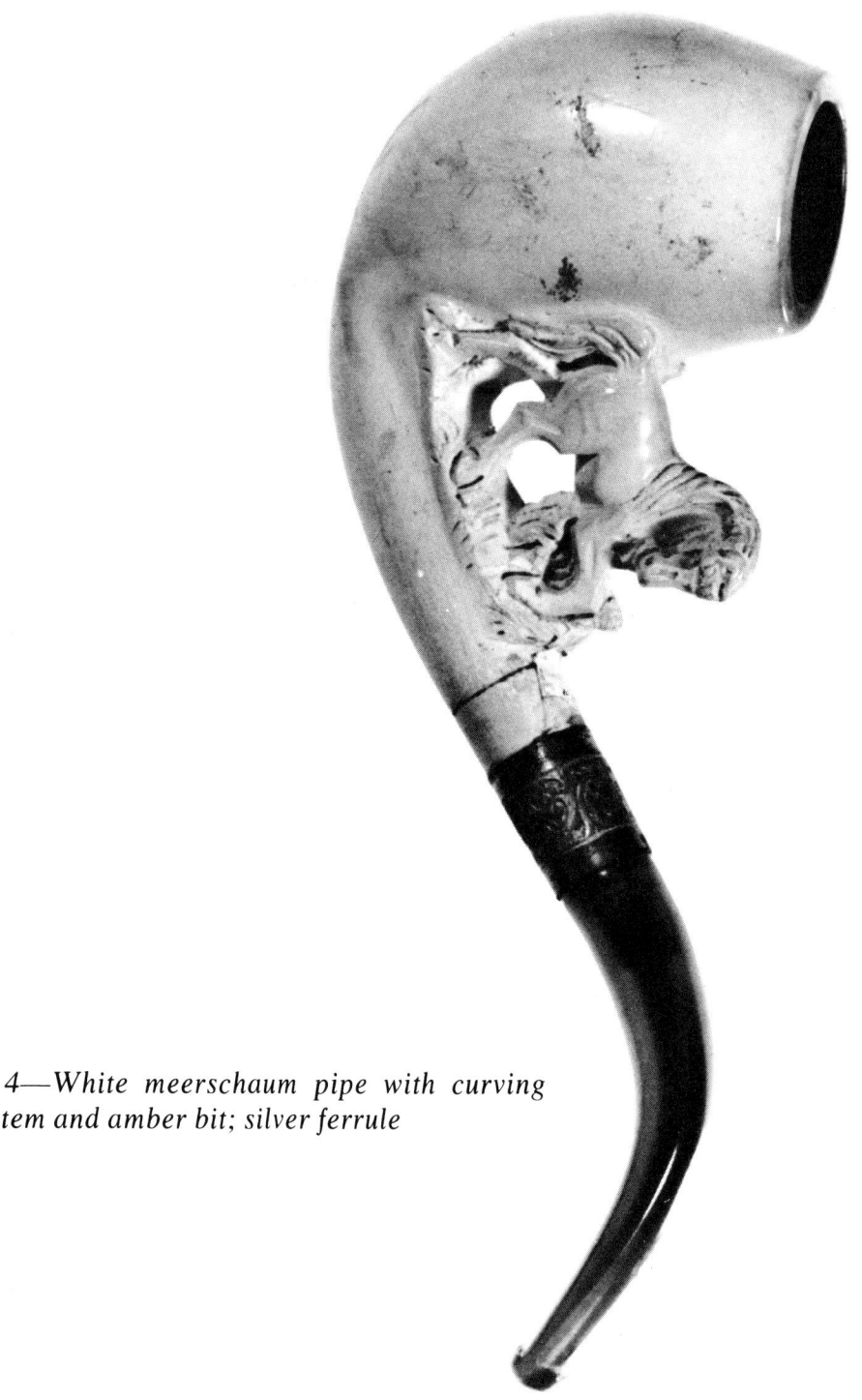

4—*White meerschaum pipe with curving stem and amber bit; silver ferrule*

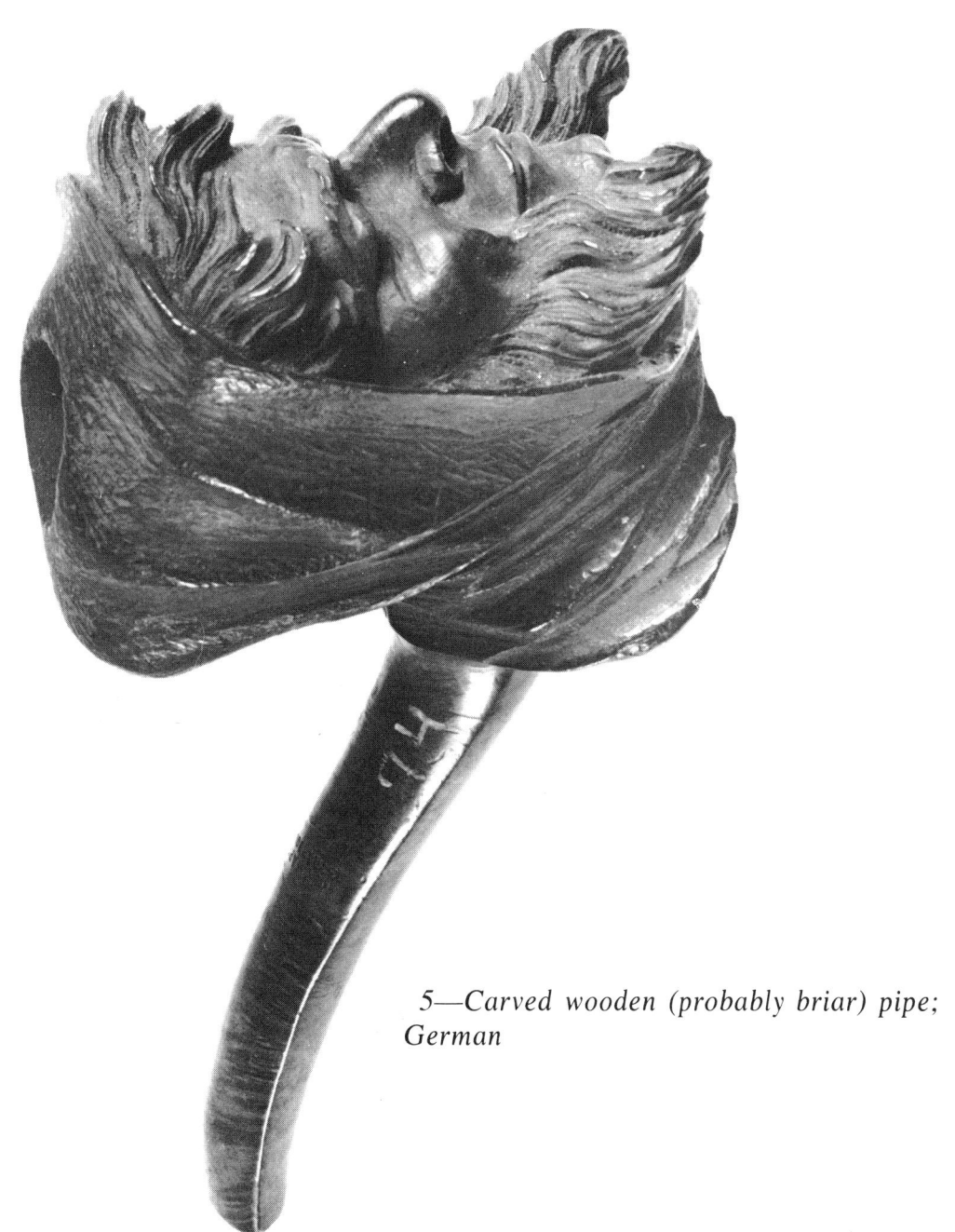

5—Carved wooden (probably briar) pipe; German

133

6—Clay pipes; French, last quarter of the 19th century

7—Pipe with carved wooden bowl with brass lid, horn stem with carved ivory section and horn bit

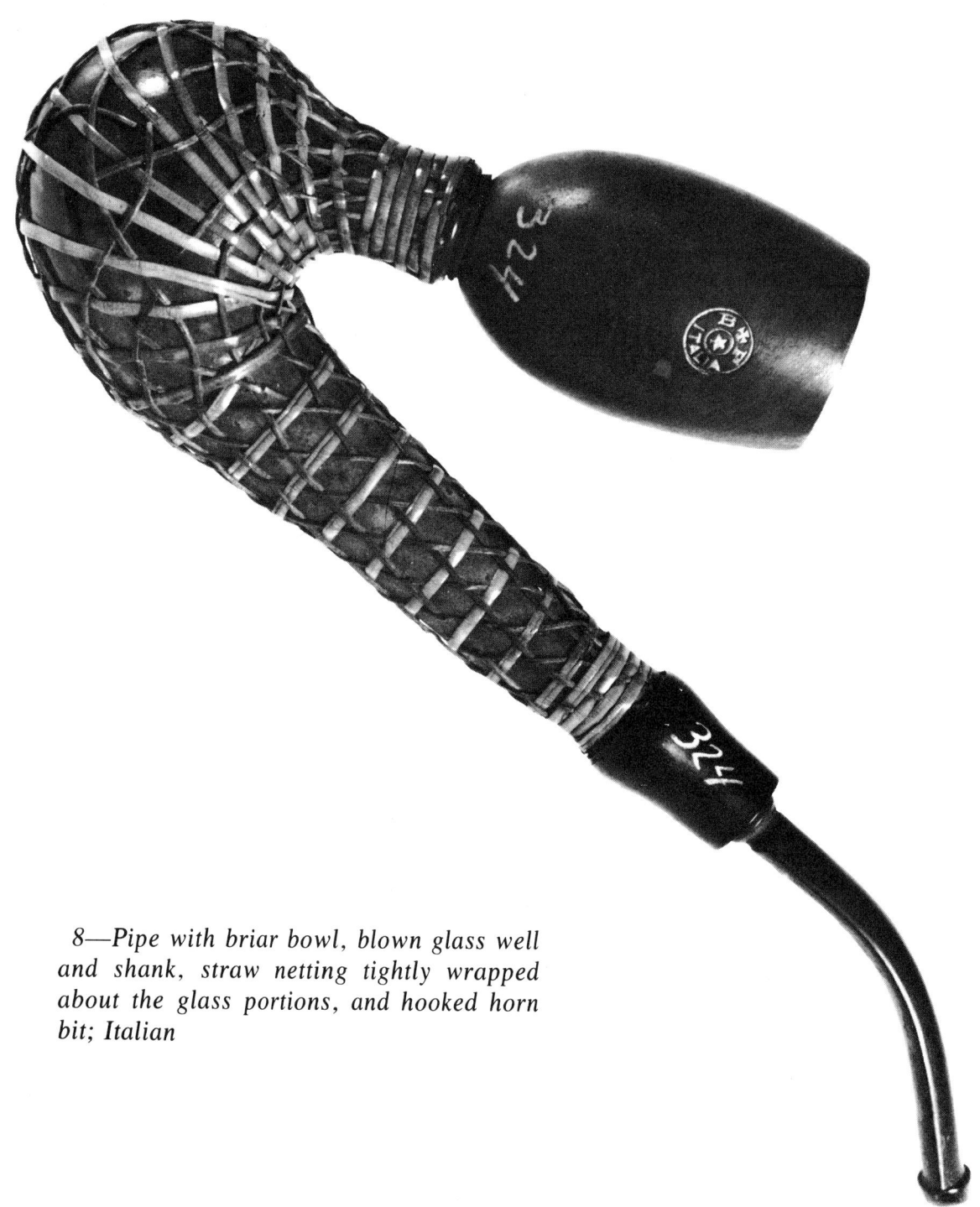

8—Pipe with briar bowl, blown glass well and shank, straw netting tightly wrapped about the glass portions, and hooked horn bit; Italian

9—*Four red clay pipe bowls*

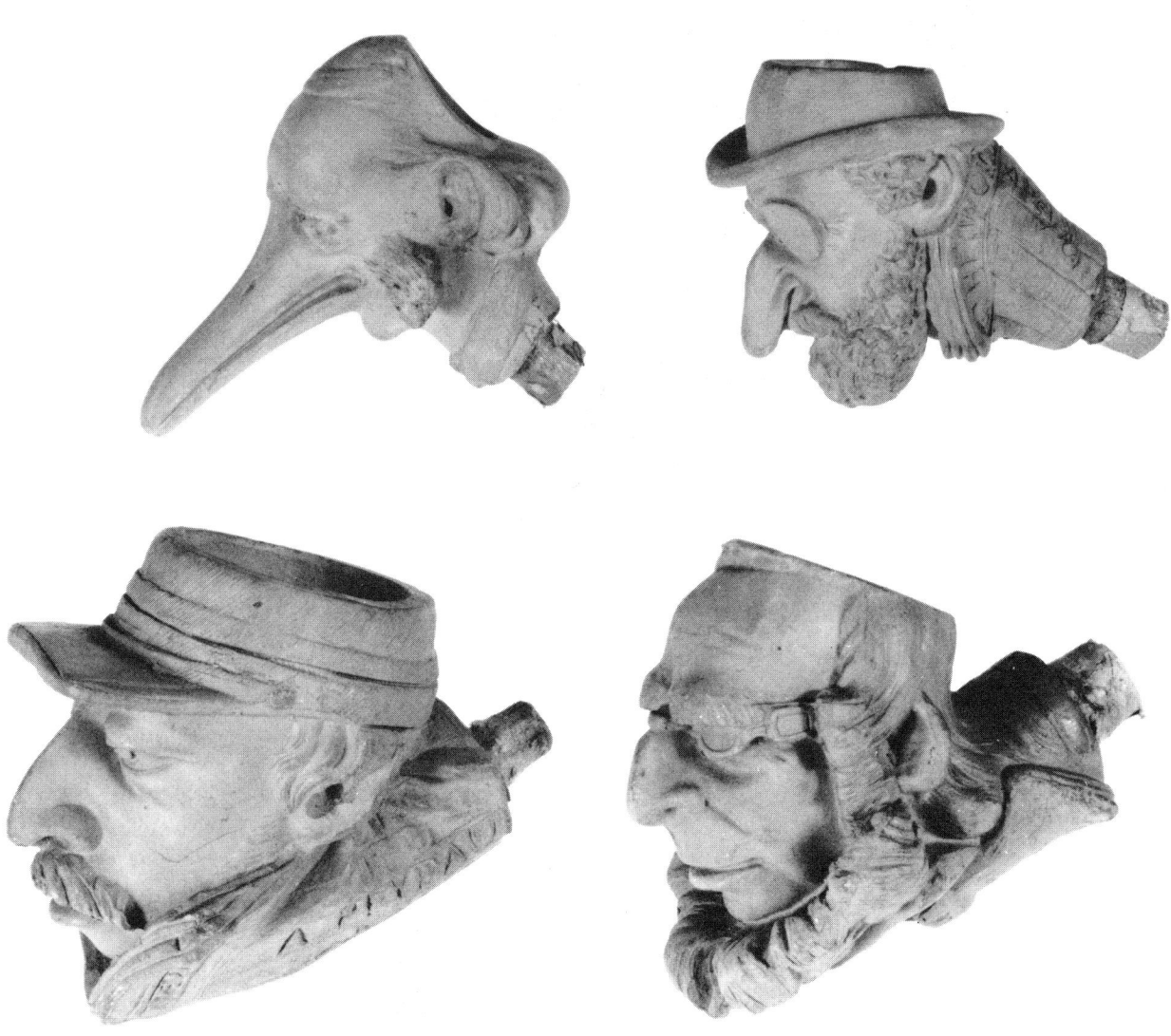

10—Meerschaum pipe with curved amber stem

11—Pipe with clay bowl in the shape of a skull with green glass eyes, and white glazed teeth; Marked: "Gambier/922/Paris

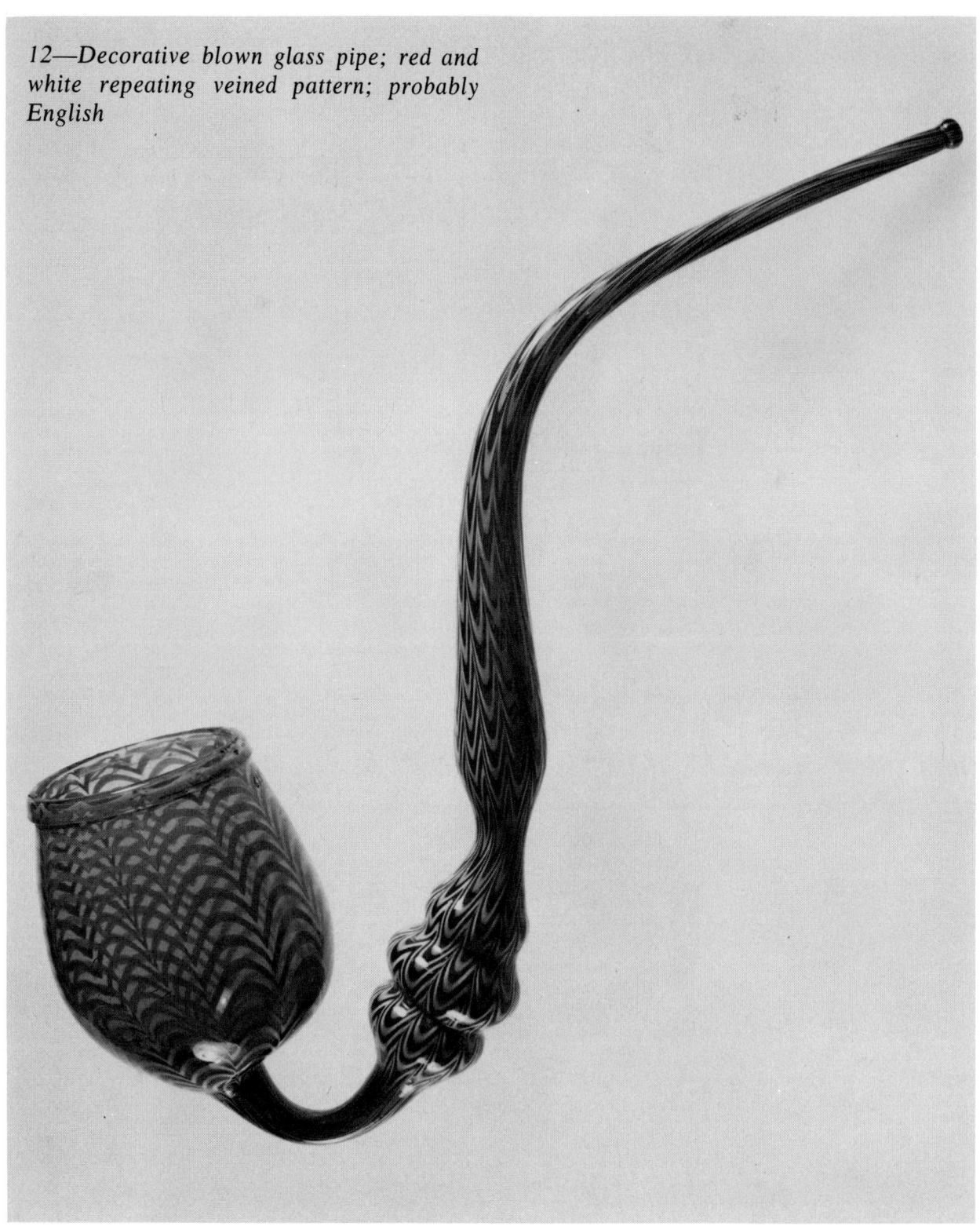

12—Decorative blown glass pipe; red and white repeating veined pattern; probably English

688   Goldring, William
Gol   The Pipe Book.

DATE DUE

HARTFORD PUBLIC LIBRARY

HARTFORD PUBLIC LIBRARY